2 of 1

West Ham United: 101 Bea.

CW00553111

To Uncle Daven
If you change your Mind
we can always go to
Arsenal together!
Love Harrison xxx

DESERT ISLAND FOOTBALL HISTORIES	ISBN
Aberdeen: A Centenary History 1903-2003	978-1-874287-57-5
Aberdeen: Champions of Scotland 1954-55	978-1-874287-65-0
Aberdeen: The European Era	978-1-905328-32-1
Bristol City: The Modern Era – A Complete Record	978-1-905328-27-7
Bristol City: From War to War 1915-1946	978-1-905328-43-7
Bristol City: The Early Years 1894-1915	978-1-874287-74-2
Bristol Rovers: The Bert Tann Era	978-1-905328-37-6
Cambridge United: The League Era – A Complete Record	978-1-905328-06-2
Cambridge United: 101 Golden Greats	978-1-874287-58-2
Carlisle United: A Season in the Sun 1974-75	978-1-905328-21-5
The Story of the Celtic 1888-1938	978-1-874287-15-5
Chelsea: Champions of England 1954-55	978-1-874287-94-0
Colchester United: Graham to Whitton – A Complete Record	978-1-905328-35-2
Colchester United: From Conference to Championship	978-1-905328-28-4
Coventry City at Highfield Road 1899-2005	978-1-905328-11-6
Coventry City: The Elite Era – A Complete Record	978-1-874287-83-4
Coventry City: An Illustrated History	978-1-874287-59-9
Coventry City: The Seven-Year Itch	978-1-905328-44-4
Derby County: Champions of England 1971-72, 1974-75	978-1-874287-98-8
Dundee: Champions of Scotland 1961-62	978-1-874287-86-5
Dundee United: Champions of Scotland 1982-83	978-1-874287-99-5
History of the Everton Football Club 1878-1928	978-1-874287-14-8
Halifax Town: From Ball to Lillis – A Complete Record	978-1-874287-26-1
Hereford United: The League Era – A Complete Record	978-1-874287-91-9
Hereford United: The Wilderness Years 1997-2006	978-1-905328-22-2
Huddersfield Town: Champions of England 1923-1926	978-1-874287-88-9
Ipswich Town: The Modern Era – A Complete Record	978-1-905328-24-6
Ipswich Town: Champions of England 1961-62	978-1-874287-63-6
The Old Farm: Ipswich Town v Norwich City	978-1-905328-12-3
Kilmarnock: Champions of Scotland 1964-65	978-1-874287-87-2
Leyton Orient: A Season in the Sun 1962-63	978-1-905328-05-5
Luton Town at Kenilworth Road: A Century of Memories	978-1-905328-10-9
Luton Town: The Modern Era – A Complete Record	978-1-874287-90-2
Luton Town: An Illustrated History	978-1-874287-79-7
Luton Town: Staring into the Abyss	978-1-905328-46-8
Manchester United's Golden Age 1903-1914: Dick Duckworth	978-1-874287-92-6
The Matt Busby Chronicles: Manchester United 1946-69	978-1-874287-96-4
Motherwell: Champions of Scotland 1931-32	978-1-874287-73-5
Northampton Town: A Season in the Sun 1965-66	978-1-905328-01-7
Norwich City: The Modern Era – A Complete Record	978-1-874287-67-4
Peterborough United: The Modern Era – A Complete Record	978-1-874287-33-9
Peterborough United: Who's Who?	978-1-874287-48-3
Plymouth Argyle: The Modern Era – A Complete Record	978-1-874287-62-9
Plymouth Argyle: 101 Golden Greats	978-1-874287-64-3
Plymouth Argyle: Snakes & Ladders – Promotions and Relegations	978-1-905328-34-5
Portsmouth: The Modern Era	978-1-905328-08-7
Portsmouth: From Tindall to Ball – A Complete Record	978-1-874287-25-4
Portsmouth: Champions of England – 1948-49 & 1949-50	978-1-874287-50-6
The Story of the Rangers 1873-1923	978-1-874287-95-7
The Romance of the Wednesday 1867-1926	978-1-874287-17-9
Seventeen Miles from Paradise: Southampton v Portsmouth	978-1-905328-41-3
The Southend United Chronicles 1906-2006	978-1-905328-18-5
Stoke City: The Modern Era – A Complete Record	978-1-905328-47-5
Stoke City: 101 Golden Greats	978-1-874287-55-1
Potters at War: Stoke City 1939-47	978-1-874287-78-0
Swansea City: Seasons in the Sun	978-1-905328-02-4
Third Lanark: Champions of Scotland 1903-04	978-1-905328-03-1
Tottenham Hotspur: Champions of England 1950-51, 1960-61	978-1-874287-93-3
West Bromwich Albion: Champions of England 1919-1920	978-1-905328-04-8
West Ham: From Greenwood to Redknapp	978-1-874287-19-3
West Ham: The Elite Era – A Complete Record	978-1-905328-33-8
West Ham: 101 Beautiful Games	978-1-905328-48-2
Hammers Through the Looking Glass	978-1-905328-23-9
Wimbledon: From Southern League to Premiership	978-1-874287-09-4
Wimbledon: From Wembley to Selhurst	978-1-874287-20-9
Wimbledon: The Premiership Years	978-1-874287-40-7
Wrexham: The European Era – A Complete Record	978-1-905328-49-9
England's Quest for the World Cup – A Complete Record	978-1-905328-16-1
Scotland: The Quest for the World Cup – A Complete Record	978-1-897850-50-3
Ireland: The Quest for the World Cup – A Complete Record	978-1-897850-80-0
Billy Walker: Once, Twice, Three Times a Winner	978-1-905328-42-0
Blinded by the Lights: A History of Night Football in England	978-1-905328-13-0
Red Dragons in Europe – A Complete Record	978-1-874287-01-8
The Book of Football: A History to 1905-06	978-1-905328-00-0
Football's Twelve Apostles: The Making of the League 1886-1889	978-1-905328-09-3
Football's War & Peace: The Tumultuous Season of 1946-47	978-1-874287-70-4

West Ham United
101 Beautiful Games

Series Editor: Clive Leatherdale

Martin Godleman

DESERT ISLAND BOOKS

First published in 2008
by
DESERT ISLAND BOOKS LIMITED
7 Clarence Road, Southend-on-Sea, Essex SS1 1AN
United Kingdom
www.desertislandbooks.com

© 2008 Martin Godleman

The right of Martin Godleman to be identified as author of this work has
been asserted under The Copyright Designs and Patents Act 1988

British Library Cataloguing-in-Publication Data
A catalogue record for this book is available from the British Library

ISBN 978-1-905328-48-2

Photographs provided by kind permission of Steve Bacon, *Newham Recorder*

Printed in Great Britain
by
4Edge Limited, Hockley, Essex

Contents

Introduction			7
1	12.12.08	Norwich 6 West Ham 3 (Southern League)	8
2	21.10.11	West Ham 7 Brentford 4 (Southern League)	9
3	31.10.14	Croydon Common 1 West Ham 2 (Southern League)	11
4	30.08.19	West Ham 1 Lincoln 1	12
5	01.01.21	West Ham 7 Coventry 0	14
6	28.04.23	Bolton 2 West Ham 0 (FA Cup final)	15
7	07.03.27	West Ham 7 Arsenal 0	18
8	21.12.29	West Ham 5 Aston Villa 2	19
9	01.09.30	West Ham 7 Liverpool 0	20
10	29.10.32	West Ham 4 Burnley 4	21
11	04.05.35	Bolton 3 West Ham 1	23
12	02.02.39	West Ham 2 Tottenham 1 (FA Cup R4 2R)	25
13	08.06.40	West Ham 1 Blackburn 0 (Football League War Cup final)	27
14	02.09.46	West Ham 3 Fulham 2	28
15	06.03.48	Birmingham 0 West Ham 1	30
16	12.01.52	West Ham 2 Blackpool 1 (FA Cup R3)	31
17	16.01.54	Fulham 3 West Ham 4	33
18	03.03.56	Tottenham 3 West Ham 3 (FA Cup QF)	35
19	26.04.58	Middlesbrough 1 West Ham 3	36
20	08.09.58	West Ham 3 Manchester United 2	38
21	31.01.59	West Ham 5 Nottingham Forest 3	41
22	05.11.60	West Ham 6 Arsenal 0	42
23	16.12.61	Manchester United 1 West Ham 2	43
24	08.09.62	Manchester City 1 West Ham 6	45
25	14.09.63	Liverpool 1 West Ham 2	46
26	02.05.64	West Ham 3 Preston 2 (FA Cup final)	48
27	19.05.65	West Ham 2 TSV Munich 1860 0 (ECWC final)	50
28	17.12.66	Chelsea 5 West Ham 5	51
29	08.09.67	Sunderland 1 West Ham 5	53
30	19.10.68	West Ham 8 Sunderland 0	54
31	02.11.68	West Ham 4 Queens Park Rangers 3	55
32	26.02.69	Mansfield 3 West Ham 0 (FA Cup R5)	56
33	11.08.69	West Ham 2 Chelsea 0	58
34	21.03.70	Manchester City 1 West Ham	59
35	05.12.70	Derby 2 West Ham 4	60
36	17.11.71	West Ham 5 Sheffield United 0 (League Cup QF)	61
37	15.12.71	West Ham 0 Stoke 1 (League Cup SF 1L)	63
38	26.01.72	Stoke 3 West Ham 2 (League Cup SF 2R)	64
39	19.08.72	West Ham 5 Leicester 2	66
40	14.04.73	West Ham 1 Leeds 1	67
41	26.12.73	Chelsea 2 West Ham 4	91
42	27.04.74	West Ham 2 Liverpool 2	92
43	16.11.74	West Ham 5 Wolverhampton 2	93
44	08.03.75	Arsenal 0 West Ham 2 (FA Cup QF)	94
45	03.05.75	West Ham 2 Fulham 0 (FA Cup final)	95
46	03.03.76	Den Haag 4 West Ham 2 (ECWC QF 1L)	97
47	14.04.76	West Ham 2 Eintracht Frankfurt 1 (ECWC SF2L)	99
48	19.02.77	Arsenal 2 West Ham 3	100

49	16.05.77	West Ham 4 Manchester United 2	101
50	08.04.78	Leeds 1 West Ham 2	102
51	04.12.79	West Ham 0 Nottingham Forest 0 (League Cup QF)	103
52	10.05.80	West Ham 1 Arsenal 0 (FA Cup final)	104
53	14.03.81	West Ham 1 Liverpool 1 (League Cup final)	106
54	02.09.81	Tottenham 0 West Ham 4	109
55	11.09.82	West Ham 5 Birmingham 0	110
56	01.01.83	West Ham 3 Tottenham 0	111
57	25.10.83	West Ham 10 Bury 0 (Milk Cup)	112
58	14.05.84	West Ham 0 Everton 1	113
59	27.10.84	West Ham 3 Arsenal 1	114
60	09.03.85	Manchester United 4 West Ham 2 (FA Cup QF)	115
61	31.08.85	West Ham 2 Liverpool 2	117
62	29.03.86	Chelsea 0 West Ham 4	118
63	21.04.86	West Ham 8 Newcastle 1	119
64	30.04.86	West Ham 2 Ipswich 1	120
65	08.04.87	West Ham 3 Arsenal 1	122
66	21.11.87	West Ham 3 Nottingham Forest 2	123
67	02.05.88	West Ham 4 Chelsea 1	125
68	30.11.88	West Ham 4 Liverpool 1 (Littlewoods Cup)	126
69	22.04.89	West Ham 3 Millwall 0	127
70	06.10.90	West Ham 7 Hull 1	127
71	11.05.91	West Ham 1 Notts County 2	128
72	22.04.92	West Ham 1 Manchester United 0	130
73	02.05.92	West Ham 3 Nottingham Forest 0	131
74	21.11.92	West Ham 5 Oxford 3	132
75	08.05.93	West Ham 2 Cambridge 0	133
76	18.09.93	Blackburn 0 West Ham 2	134
77	04.04.94	Tottenham 1 West Ham 4	135
78	17.12.94	West Ham 3 Manchester City 0	136
79	14.05.95	West Ham 1 Manchester United 1	137
80	31.01.96	West Ham 3 Coventry 2	139
81	23.03.96	West Ham 4 Manchester City 2	141
82	24.02.97	West Ham 4 Tottenham 3	142
83	27.09.97	West Ham 2 Liverpool 1	144
84	10.01.98	West Ham 6 Barnsley 0	145
85	09.09.98	West Ham 3 Wimbledon 4	147
86	24.08.99	FC Metz 1 West Ham 3 (Inter Toto Cup F2L)	148
87	03.10.99	West Ham 2 Arsenal 1	150
88	12.02.00	West Ham 5 Bradford City 4	152
89	26.12.00	West Ham 5 Charlton 0	155
90	28.01.01	Manchester United 0 West Ham 1 (FA Cup)	156
91	19.11.01	Charlton 4 West Ham 4	158
92	28.09.02	Chelsea 2 West Ham 3	159
93	03.05.03	West Ham 1 Chelsea 0	161
94	12.05.04	West Ham 2 Ipswich 0 (Play-off SF 2L)	163
95	18.05.05	Ipswich 0 West Ham 2 (Play-off SF 2L)	165
96	31.01.06	Arsenal 2 West Ham 3	166
97	13.05.06	West Ham 3 Liverpool 3 (FA Cup final)	167
98	13.05.07	Manchester United 0 West Ham 1	169
99	29.12.07	West Ham 2 Manchester United 1	170
100	15.03.08	West Ham 2 Blackburn 1	172
101	29.08.08	West Ham 4 Blackburn 1	173

INTRODUCTION

Triumph over adversity, victory against the odds, backs against the wall, hope over experience … the images easily collate to chronicle yet another 90 minutes of football involving West Ham United.

The teams may run out the same way each week, the goalkeepers kicking the ball high in the air towards the corner where they'll be spending the next 45 minutes. It's of no material relevance. Seasons have come and gone when the expression 'Fortress Upton Park' could be uttered in all seriousness – until an amateur side somehow force a third round FA Cup replay. Then a season where the opening twenty minutes of any home game will invariably yield an opposition goal or two without reply, and they turn over Manchester United 3-0 without breaking stride. That's what it's like being a West Ham supporter – and I am, so I know.

Picking 101 games from the last 101 years wouldn't be easy if I had been alive the whole time. Only having lived for less than half that term, it's a task that is always going to be entirely personal. Cup finals and giant-killing achievements have to make the cut, as they are golden out of rarity, but plucking 90-odd battles from upwards of 3,500 is a delicious but ultimately unsatisfying task. I will have missed many that you would insist upon including – I may not have seen the game in question or felt sympathy with its constituent parts – it might have been one of those unusual periods when I completely lost interest in football, temporarily …

There are good reasons for each of the 101 games occupying this book, as will soon become evident. They tell of never-to-be-forgotten encounters and in their own strange way provide a developing narrative to the unquantifiable tapestry that is the West Ham supporter's backdrop. If you are one of those rare creatures – a football fan without a team – you may find a tiny tugging temptation to spend an afternoon at Upton Park in the flesh to try on the experience for size. I can positively recommend it as a one-size-fits-all sporting experience.

NOTE: At the end of each match, West Ham team line-ups are provided, plus a personal choice of Man of the Match (MoM).

Number: 1	1908-09:	Southern League (1)
12th December 1908	Norwich City (a)	Att: 4,500

NORWICH 6 WEST HAM 3

West Ham, despite a travelling defensive reputation that has endured for over a century, rarely concede six goals in a game. This match at Carrow Road was only the second time in West Ham's history where they'd scored three goals and still managed to end up on the losing side. Their inside-right, Billy Grassam, had also been involved in the previous one, 3-4 at Portsmouth in October 1906, where he'd scored a hat-trick. As you will come to realise, the Hammers are no strangers to goal-gluts.

Norwich City had only been formed six years earlier when they faced the travelling Hammers, but they had been singing their own song since their inception. Imaginatively titled 'On the Ball, City', it is thought to be the oldest football ditty still in use anywhere in the world, over 100 years later.

1908-09 was shaping up to be West Ham's worst season in the Southern League, under their relatively new guise, as the campaign entered December. They'd won just six of their first sixteen matches (all at home) as they faced Norwich at Carrow Road. Norwich were actually below them in the table and looked a bit of a pushover at that point, especially as they played their games in a disused chalk pit.

Norwich took the lead early on from a penalty by Tommy Allsop, but in a rush of blood the Hammers threw caution to the three winds, or however many there are in East Anglia, and hit three goals in quick succession, John Burton hitting two – before a third – a powerful volley by Billy Grassam. Herbert Ashton could claim a hand in the moves that led to all three goals, and throughout the first half he was the pick of the West Ham players. Hammers got to half-time with their 3-1 goal cushion intact, on course for their first away win of the season. If the forwards had taken advantage of the many crosses from Ashton and Blackburn, the Hammers might have been out of sight.

Not for nothing was 'a game of two halves' coined as football's least favourite cliché. It reverberated around the chalk pit for most of the second half as Norwich's forwards rained in shots on poor George Kitchen, and it wasn't long before they started getting past him. Ten minutes from the end Norwich had scored five without reply and ran out 6-3 winners, despite being behind for over half the game.

Poor Hammers failed to win a single away win throughout the season, but after throwing away a lead as spectacularly as they did at Carrow

Road, it was hardly surprising. Not only that, but three days later Bob Young was sold to Middlesbrough for £500.

In a 40-match season, Norwich scored a tenth of their season's output in this one game. Hammers also conceded six at Northampton at the end of February; not a great season to face teams whose name began with 'N' (though Northampton had the decency to win the league that season).

1 George Kitchen, 2 James Gault, 3 Fred Shreeve, 4 Bob Young, 5 Frank Piercy (capt), 6 Len Jarvis, 7 Herbert Ashton, 8 Billy Grassam, 9 Jack Foster, 10 John Burton, 11 Fred Blackburn.

Scorers: John Burton 2, Billy Grassam
MoM: Herbert Ashton
West Ham ended the season: 17th out of 21, with 36 points.

Number: 2	1911-12	Southern League (1)
21st October 1911	Brentford (h)	Att: 10,000

WEST HAM 7 BRENTFORD 4

West Ham were already building a reputation for being a young professional side more than capable of 'mixing it' with those from the Football League. They had knocked out three First Division teams in their Cup run to the quarter-finals the previous season – Nottingham Forest, Preston North End and Manchester United. In the day-to-day business of the Southern League, however, they faced Brentford, having drawn four of their opening seven games. Two defeats and a single win – 5-0 against Reading – represented a pretty poor start to the season, but the fans at Upton Park on an overcast day in late October 1911 would now witness a club record eleven-goal extravaganza that they would not forget in a while.

Three goals came and went in the first ten minutes. Willis Rippon netted the first for Brentford, but Danny Shea equalised and Bill Kennedy scored three minutes later to put the Hammers in front. Not content with three in ten minutes, Danny Shea hit two more to complete his hat-trick, both powerful shots from the edge of the area, and Hammers were 4-1 up in the first half-hour.

Brentford scored a second through Rippon after Geggus had fumbled a cross from Anderson, but two minutes before the interval Bill Kennedy scored his second of the match to take the Hammers into the break with a remarkble 5-2 scoreline.

As if that wasn't entertainment enough, there were to be another four goals in the second half. Hendren pulled it back to 5-3 with a third for Brentford before Kennedy completed his hat-trick and Fred Harrison added another to make it seven for West Ham. Incredibly, Brentford hadn't quite finished and Rippon got his hat-trick for Brentford with the final goal of the match near the end to make the score 7-4. He had just been transferred from Woolwich Arsenal and had arrived at the club the day before. Quite a debut, away from home, scoring three in your first game, and still ending up on the losing side. Whether or not Rippon is related to Angela Rippon, who Brentford fan Greg Dyke appointed to his TV-am channel in the 1980s, is for the moment unclear.

West Ham would spend a further three years in the Southern League because of the intervention of the Great War, so finishing the 1911-12 season in 13th position was a huge disappointment after a finish of 5th the previous season. Danny Shea, however, once again topped the goalscorers at the club with 24 goals, his previous seasons' tallies being 28 and 31 respectively. Not bad for a player discovered by West Ham coach Charlie Paynter playing football for the Stratford pub team the Builders Arms in 1908.

It was a significant season for others in the side, too: George Webb became the first West Ham player to win an international cap for England on 14th March 1911. England beat Wales 3-0 that day and Webb scored one of the goals. Webb also played in the game against Scotland (1-1) on 1st April 1911, but missed West Ham's 7-4 win over Brentford due to injury, one of only three games he missed in the first eleven. Later in the season Webb was transferred to Manchester City. Frank Piercy began the season as the first Hammer to accrue 200 appearances, though he was replaced by Tommy Randall as captain in August. A few months on from his hat-trick against Brentford, Bill Kennedy suffered a serious knee injury in West Ham's FA Cup-tie against Middlesbrough on 8th February 1912 and never played professional football again.

1 John Geggus, 2 Jim Rothwell, 3 Horace Glover, 4 Bill Whiteman, 5 Fred Massey, 6 Tom Randall (capt), 7 Herbert Ashton, 8 Danny Shea, 9 Bill Kennedy, 10 Fred Harrison, 11 Jack Morrison.

Scorers: Bill Kennedy 3, Danny Shea 3, Fred Harrison
MoM: Danny Shea
West Ham ended the season: 13th out of 20, with 33 points.

Number: 3   1914-15   Southern League (1)
31st October 1914   Croydon Common (a)   Att: 5,000

CROYDON COMMON 1 WEST HAM 2

It still seems hard to believe that West Ham United once played Croydon Common in a professional football match. Can you imagine today's over-priced Upton Park set descending on the White Horse pub car park, changing in the toilets and then running out to cheers from stationary lorry drivers in jams around Selhurst Road, staring from their cabs across at the spectacle?

The 1914-15 season was the last football could offer before the Great War put a halt to most sporting events for a good five years, but it was a chance for Croydon Common, newly promoted from Division Two of the Southern League, to ply their trade against their more famous south-ern cousins from the elite section of the Southern League. One of those cousins was East End's finest London export, the Irons. Their first and last home game against the Hammers was played on the afternoon of Halloween 1914 in front of a quarter-full ground where battle took place.

History records that West Ham took the lead when inside-right Dan Bailey forced his way into the Croydon penalty area and flicked the ball home, one of the few events in a fairly tepid first half.

In the second half, the equaliser, like a tardy bus held up by unex-pected roadworks, arrived on the scene. Taking advantage of an unchar-acteristic but symmetrical hesitation by Frank Burton and Joe Webster, Ryder dashed between them and scored to bring rapture to the home fans. West Ham, however, promptly regained the lead when Jack Casey's acceleration down the wing and telling ball found captain Alf Leafe, who gratefully pounced on the perfect pass to force the ball home. The Croydon Common crowd – and there were 5,000 of them – unexpect-edly robbed of their élan, lost their heads and began to yell abuse at the poor referee, convinced that Leafe had been offside. After one of the Common players, Williamson, suffered a serious knock and was forced to leave the field, the semi-rioting fans' further irritation blossomed. And in the midst of all this, there followed ruminations on another missed opportunity for Syd Puddefoot to score away from home – he scored eighteen goals that season, but only two on the road. At least he had been selected to represent the Southern League in an upcoming fixture against the First Division League. The game ended with the referee being escort-ed from the pitch by two burly policemen, keen that he should not become human pork scratchings to the now baying crowd.

While all this was going on, West Ham reserves were playing their own fixture at Upton Park, and turned over Croydon Common reserves 7-0, the diminutive Arthur Stallard scoring five in addition to goals from George Butcher and Jack Mackesy.

In 1917 Croydon Common were wound up, the only First Division club from the Southern League not to return to action after the Great War, after a history of just twenty years. A year later Crystal Palace began playing on the Croydon Common athletic ground ('The Nest') for the next six years before moving to their current stadium at Selhurst Park. The ground has since become a very sad and simple siding for Southern trains not intending to go any further than Selhurst or Norwood Junction stations.

1 Joe Webster, 2 Frank Burton, 3 Alf Tirrell, 4 Bill Whiteman, 5 Billy Askew, 6 Alf Fenwick, 7 Harry Caton, 8 Dan Bailey, 9 Syd Puddefoot, 10 Alf Leafe (capt), 11 Jack Casey.

Scorers: Dan Bailey, Alf Leafe
MoM: Dan Bailey
West Ham ended the season: 4th out of 20, with 45 points.

| Number: 4 | 1919-20 | Division 2 |
| 30th August 1919 | Lincoln City (h) | Att: 20,000 |

WEST HAM 1 LINCOLN 1

1919-20 was West Ham's first season in the Football League (Division Two) and their first since the Great War. They managed to acquire League status thanks to their impressive record in the London Combination leagues during the war, applying to join the League following the Armistice of November 1918, and given their new status the following March.

Making his debut for the Hammers in their first ever league game was goalkeeper Ted 'Tiger' Hufton who had already guested for the club during the war. Hammers' new captain, tough-tackling defender Bill Cope, was signed from Oldham in 1914. He was soon preparing his team to take on Lincoln in their red and white striped shirts and black silky knickers (as reported in the *Stratford Express*). The game itself posed unexpected changes for the fans with admission prices double what they had been in the Southern League, but Hammers still fielded 20,000.

Hammers' man of the moment, Syd Puddefoot, found himself close-ly marked by Ormiston, the old Chelsea half-back. Whenever he wasn't being given offside, he was being shoulder-charged so roughly that he had to head to the touchline on more than one occasion for a dose of the 'magic sponge'. The West Ham wingers were quick, Bob Morris the best of the inside-forwards on show. Lincoln's centre-forward Egerton caused the Hammers' defence problems, as did McCulloch, who almost got through several times in the first half. There was a moment halfway through the first half when Puddefoot dribbled along the right and pulled the ball back for Morris, who missed it by a whisker with the goal gaping. Fenwick played well at centre-half, deputising for the absent Kay. Whenever Egerton threatened to get through, Fenwick was in the way to put a stop to the attack. Lincoln were unlucky when Chesser saw his cross-shot crash against the bar with Hufton well beaten, but at the other end, with Puddefoot through and taking aim, he lost his footing in the mud. Morris tried something they called, in those days, a 'screw shot', but for all that, it went wide.

Lincoln finally took the lead towards the end of the first half after being awarded a penalty when Bradshaw was brought down. It was such a blatant penalty that neither the crowd nor the players offered a whisper of complaint. Chesser scored from the kick, placing the ball comfortably wide of Hufton.

Hammers' never-say-die attitude pulled them back into the game after the restart. Neither side were too keen to lose the first game of the season, and when West Ham's Bradshaw won the ball in midfield and passed to Morris, the inside-right crossed to Jim Moyes who headed home West Ham's first ever league goal. Late in the game Hufton saved well from McCulloch and Chesser, so both teams could end up pleased with their first point of this new Football League season.

Syd King had a modern sounding 39 players at his disposal, but the manager was cautious in his first league season, Hammers scoring just 47 goals, the same number of points they accrued in their 42 matches, conceding only 40. This was particularly impressive after losing 0-7 in their second ever league game, at Barnsley, and by the end of the season their top goalscorer had hit over half their goals (26) in just 43 games. Early days for the Hammers, but a finish of 7th out of 22 was an impressive start to their league history.

1 Ted Hufton, 2 Bill Cope (capt), 3 Alf Lee, 4 Harry Lane, 5 Alf Fenwick, 6 Jimmy McCrae, 7 David Smith, 8 Jim Moyes, 9 Syd Puddefoot, 10 Bob Morris, 11 Harry Bradshaw.

Scorer: Jim Moyes
MoM: Bill Cope, Manager: Syd King
West Ham ended the season: 7th out of 22, with 47 points.

| Number: 5 | 1920-21 | Division 2 |
| 1st January 1921 | Coventry City (h) | Att: 8,000 |

WEST HAM 7 COVENTRY 0

1920-21 was the season that Syd King tightened up the West Ham defence (they conceded two goals on just five occasions that year – the second best record in the league) and tweaked that goalscoring machine Puddefoot to reach even greater heights with 29 goals at the end of the season. There were three particular games in which his goalscoring prowess was in evidence; the first was in November against Sheffield Wednesday when he hit all four goals in a 4-0 thrashing of the Yorkshire club. Early the following year Puddefoot was again amongst the goals, scoring all three in the 3-0 demolition of Leeds. Perhaps he had something against Yorkshire clubs, but it was certainly striking of the highest quality in his penultimate season for the Hammers. His finest effort and, indeed, that of the club during 1920-21 came in the New Year's Day home fixture against Coventry.

Coventry had been having a poor season, not surprising in those days, rarely gaining away points, and on this occasion they met Hammers after two tough games against champions Birmingham. On fire against Coventry were Puddefoot and Alf Leafe (who had scored a hat-trick against Stockport in November), Hammers setting about the Midlanders from the first minute.

West Ham's forwards' 'shooting ability' had been questioned as they had only scored more than two goals twice that year. Today, all that was to change. If Coventry's Best hadn't been in such fine form, Hammers might have run up twenty goals. The turf was muddy and slippery, and it was soon obvious that the first side to master the conditions would run rings round the other.

Syd Puddefoot was a king of the dribble, perfection in his mastery of the ball that afternoon. In the first minute there came a goal that would have been a contender for Goal of the Decade, had such a prize existed. Leafe gathered a neat pass from Kay and, 30 yards out, beat Best with a left-foot rocket that hit the back of the net with the sound of Leafe's foot striking it still in everybody's ears. There followed a 25-minute virtuoso performance of goalkeeping defiance as Best made every kind of save imaginable. After 26 minutes, like a failed physicist, he ran out of time and space and conceded a second when Puddefoot headed in a centre from John Young. Puddefoot shortly afterwards hit his second, and West Ham's third, struck from 25 yards. Coventry were relieved to hear the referee's whistle for half-time.

In the second half West Ham became too hot to handle, Leafe hitting a fourth, followed by Bishop making it 5-0. That would have been exciting enough, but there was another spectacle remaining as Puddefoot scored his third and fourth goals to give West Ham a 7-0 lead. Hufton had two saves to make all match and, strangely, they were both in the last ten minutes, from Dougall and Wynn.

Syd King had 35 players in his squad during 1920-21, another example of players' wages being as sheds to today's mansions.

1 Ted Hufton, 2 Frank Burton, 3 Bill Cope (capt), 4 Percy Allen, 5 George Kay, 6 Jack Tresadern, 7 George Carter, 8 Syd Bishop, 9 Syd Puddefoot, 10 Alf Leafe, 11 John Young.

Scorers: Syd Puddefoot 4, Alf Leafe 2, Syd Bishop
MoM: Syd Puddefoot
West Ham ended the season: 4th out of 22, with 48 points.

Number: 6	1922-23	FA Cup final
28th April 1923	Bolton (Wembley)	Att: 126,047

BOLTON 2 WEST HAM 0

West Ham's first appearance in an FA Cup final could not have been more dramatic, notwithstanding the fact that it was the first ever Wembley final. Hammers were on a run of form that saw them beaten only once, from 11th November to 16th April, against Barnsley. They went into the final with two league games to play and, with Manchester United and Leicester hot on their heels, knew that they would probably have to get points from both of them. That, however, would have to be put on the back burner until the Monday night.

Fronted by the greatest ever West Ham striker, Vic Watson (27 goals), and his sidekick Billy Moore (20), the Hammers knew they should fear nobody. For three seasons in a row they had been close to promotion, but this time looked like finally succeeding, and with the bonus of a cup final appearance it was unquestionably the greatest season in West Ham's history to date.

The journey to the 1923 FA Cup final was widely reported as fraught with trepidation due to the number of spectators turning up and the officials' inability to safely police them. It had been thought that with both clubs having average home attendances of around 20,000, the stadium's 125,000 capacity would be comfortably sufficient. How wrong they were. All that stood between safety and a Hillsborough-style disaster was the fact that most people managed to get in after the iron entrance gates were smashed. And as the turnstiles were locked and deserted, the crowds just climbed over them. People's behaviour was surprisingly cordial on the day, and somehow the majority of the fans eventually squeezed into the ground, the police on duty forming a human chain to keep them back from the pitch so the match could go ahead. The final may have been called the 'White Horse' final because of PC George Scorey and his famous white horse Billie, but it was probably the other 40 or 50 horses that did the balance of the work, keeping the crowd back.

The game, once under way, was brought to a halt on several occasions in the first few minutes whenever the police couldn't take the strain and had to break their human chain so that people spilled on to the pitch, but after a while the fans held themselves back as best they could, aware that without restraint the game would have been abandoned. West Ham's wingers were clearly inhibited by the proximity of the crowd to the pitch, unable to fly off down the wing as they liked to do, and they had to play more of a short-passing game than kick and run, which naturally favoured the Bolton players. The other problem was the edge of the pitch itself which had great divots, ruts and holes that the players kept tripping over. It was a wonder no one twisted an ankle or broke a leg.

The first goal came after six minutes, when Ted Vizard, the Bolton Welsh international, found Joe Smith after an exchange of passes. Smith hit a long ball to David Jack, who took on and beat Tresadern and Young before hitting a shot into the top corner past Ted Hufton's outstretched hands.

It was a considerable setback to concede a goal so early on, and it was a while before West Ham got their momentum back, Watson and Moore linking well to force a corner. Unfortunately, when it came over from the right to Watson, he ballooned the ball over the bar from five yards. Syd Bishop then forced Pym to his knees to fumble away his powerful shot as Hammers pushed for an equaliser. Bolton then had a second goal disallowed after Butler's ball from Vizard's centre was pushed through to Smith who turned it in, but was given offside.

At half-time, and with no realistic chance of escaping to the changing rooms, the two sides changed ends and kicked off straight away. Early in the second half West Ham carved out another scoring opportunity, Richards crossing from the right and the ball sailing across the goal about chest high, just out of the reach of Watson, to Bolton keeper Pym's relief. Shortly afterwards Bolton managed to break away after a West Ham attack, and from an ensuing right-wing cross, Joe Smith, the Bolton captain, beat West Ham's George Kay to the ball and hit it on the half volley just inside the right-hand post to give Bolton a 2-0 lead. The occasion and the weariness as the final whistle approached were just too much for the Hammers, who boldly attempted to overcome the opposition and mount attacks but ended up just keeping the opposition at bay for the closing minutes.

Once the whistle went, both teams were presented to the King, and Bolton paraded the Cup on a lap of honour. There were suggestions that West Ham should lodge a protest about the fact that throw-ins could not be taken as the crowd spilled over the touchline, but despite the fact that they might have had a case, the club said the game was played in good spirits and the result should stand. Very different to the kind of reaction that would most likely happen today, one imagines.

West Ham may have lost the cup final, but their 2-0 win at Sheffield Wednesday two days later set them up for an intriguing last game against Notts County at home on 5th May, a fixture whose significance would be echoed in a similar situation in May 1991 (game number 71), 68 years later. This time it was the same issue – West Ham had to win to be certain of the Second Division Championship. Leicester were playing at Bury earlier in the day. If Leicester lost, then both County and West Ham would be promoted; if they won and Hammers and County drew, then West Ham would go up on goal-average.

The only way West Ham could fail to get promotion would be if they lost and Leicester won. Unfortunately, Hammers fell behind seven minutes before half-time, but as they struggled to find an equaliser in the second half, news reached the ground that Leicester had lost! The remaining minutes were played out in knockabout style and both clubs celebrated their promotion at the end of the match.

The Empire Stadium had been built by Sir Robert McAlpine for the 1923 British Empire Exhibition, but instead of demolishing it at the end, it was decided to keep it to host football matches. The building was only completed four days before the final – some things never change. Despite the incredible number of fans turning up for the final, the next game at Wembley, England v Scotland, was only attended by 37,250 people.

1 Ted Hufton, 2 Billy Henderson, 3 John Young, 4 Syd Bishop, 5 George Kay (capt), 6 Jack Tresadern, 7 Dick Richards, 8 Billy Brown, 9 Victor Watson, 10 Billy Moore, 11 Jimmy Ruffell.

MoM: George Kay
West Ham ended the season: 2nd out of 22, with 51 points (promoted behind Notts County with 53 points).

Number: 7	1926-27	Division 1
7th March 1927	Arsenal (h)	Att: 28,000

WEST HAM 7 ARSENAL 0

This was West Ham's fourth season in Division One and, despite two unlucky 13ths and an 18th in their first three, 1926-27 would be their best league season for decades to come. A 4-0 victory over Manchester United and a 5-1 thrashing of Aston Villa were great Upton Park performances, but it was the home fixture against 'The' Arsenal that intrigues most from that campaign.

Displaying all-round superiority and a confidence rarely seen that season, West Ham proceeded to take Arsenal apart. It wasn't that their record against them had hitherto been anything but vastly superior, it was just the manner and ease with which the Hammers took control of the match that impressed.

Hammers went ahead after six minutes with a goal created when Butler lost the ball in midfield and Ruffell took it on, beginning a run of a third of the field before looking out for Victor Watson, who hit the ball as it reached him and saw it buried in the back of the net a split second later.. Watson scored a second twenty minutes into the match, getting on the end of one Tommy Yews' perfectly weighted crosses. Jimmy Ruffell's crisp drive from just inside the area made it three. The fourth goal was so unfortunate that Hammers' fans could easily have felt some pity for Arsenal's Bob John. But they didn't. Diverting Earle's well-struck ball across the goal into his own net, Arsenal's unfortunate John failed to realise that this was hardly the time to add more suffering to his team's woes. Thankfully he only had to suffer another few minutes of guilt before the referee's whistle sent them all to the dressing rooms.

Ten minutes after the interval, Joe Johnson nipped between two Arsenal defenders to plant the ball past Lewis, which was a little rough as he had just made a stunning save from the industrious Ruffell. Arsenal were nearly as bad in attack as they were in defence, their two best moments coming within a five-minute spell, and neither yielding anything that remotely had the hallmark of 'goal' stamped on it. Hammers scored a sixth when Watson took a pass from Ruffell without breaking step and hammered it past the Arsenal stooge. Arsenal helped Hammers reach seven when right-back Parker threw himself into the path of Earle's goal-bound shot with Lewis ready to save, only to see the ball trickle past him as he fell into the unforgiving mud, wrong-footed.

A great victory, but a strange and very unusual season, West Ham managing more away wins (ten) than home ones (nine). What they wouldn't give today for a 7-0 over Arsenal!

1 David Baillie, 2 Jack Hebden (capt), 3 George Horler, 4 Jimmy Collins, 5 Jim Barrett, 6 Albert Cadwell, 7 Tommy Yews, 8 Stan Earle, 9 Victor Watson, 10 Joe Johnson, 11 Jimmy Ruffell.

Scorers: Watson (3), Johnson, Ruffell, Parker (og), John (og)
MoM: Vic Watson
West Ham ended the season: 6th out of 22, with 46 points.

| Number: 8 | 1929-30 | Division 1 |
| 21st December 1929 | Aston Villa (h) | Att: 18,000 |

WEST HAM 5 ASTON VILLA 2

1929-30 was another memorable season for West Ham. Despite Sheffield Wednesday running away with the league by a clear ten points, Hammers were always in the hunt for second place, but finished seventh after losing two of their last five games. Their finest achievement that season was Victor Watson's finish of 42 goals, making him the top goalscorer in the First Division.

The match that saw the team produce their best football was against Aston Villa at the beginning of the Christmas break. Villa had managed three top-four finishes in succession and were well organised and difficult to beat at Villa Park and on the road.

The Upton Park pitch was in its standard December condition, a bog prepared by rain since daybreak and best marshalled by those in home claret and blue, whose speed and organisation was too much for their Midland opponents. One of their most effective players, outside-left Chester, sustained an ankle injury midway through the first half, and

Smart had to leave the pitch before the end with a thigh strain, but Hammers had established their superiority long before either event.

Hobson deputised for Earle at inside-right and was far and away the star Hammer of the afternoon. His pass in the eighth minute sent Yews away past Tate on the right to deliver a perfect cross for Gibbins to head home. West Ham nearly had a second a minute later when Villa keeper Olney slipped in the mud and missed a back pass, defender Talbot just chasing back in time to hoof the ball off the line. In the 27th minute Watson scored his first after Olney had only punched out Ruffell's powerful shot. Villa's opening goal came from Brown in the 43rd minute from a penalty awarded after a supposed trip on their inside-forward Walker. It was hotly disputed by the home crowd.

In the second half Watson returned Ruffell's earlier effort by setting him up to score West Ham's third. Three minutes later Ruffell returned the compliment with a pass to put Watson through for his second goal. Watson completed his hat-trick ten minutes later after a run past three defenders, finishing with an angled shot into the corner of the Villa net. Brown scored a belated second for Villa with a penalty towards the end, after another contentiously awarded spot-kick. No matter.

1 Ted Hufton, 2 Alf Earl, 3 Charles Cox, 4 Fred Norris, 5 Jim Barrett, 6 Albert Cadwell, 7 Tommy Yews, 8 George Robson, 9 Victor Watson, 10 Vivian Gibbins, 11 Jimmy Ruffell.

Scorers: Vivian Gibbins 8, Vic Watson 27, 59, 69, Jimmy Ruffell 56
MoM: George Robson
West Ham ended the season: 7th out of 22, with 43 points.

Number: 9   Season: 1930-31   Division 1
1st September 1930   Liverpool (h)   Att: 14,000

WEST HAM 7 LIVERPOOL 0

This was the famous season when West Ham scored fifteen goals in five games, yet only won one of them. This match at Upton Park was the second game of the season, played on a Monday night, Hammers already having won their opener two days earlier against Huddersfield 2-1.

Hammers were in sublime form, quicker to the ball and the half-backs supporting the forwards throughout, supplying defence-splitting passes, many of which resulted in goal opportunities. Oddly enough, Liverpool's best chance in the game fell in the first minute when Dixon was forced to tip a swerving shot from Smith over the bar. Two minutes later they were behind. An inswinging corner-kick from Jimmy Ruffell was met perfectly and headed into the roof of the net by the captain Stan Earle. After five minutes they were two up when Watson ran on to Barrett's through ball before tucking it neatly past Riley in the Liverpool goal. West Ham then threatened to overrun Liverpool but strangely failed to add to their two-goal lead before half-time.

Early in the second half Watson hit a similar strike from Barrett's pass. Earle hit number four with his second goal of the match, after a mazy run in which he beat five different Liverpool players, including the keeper, before slipping the ball into the unguarded net.

Confusion in the Liverpool defence after a subsequent Hammers' attack presented Billy James with a tap-in finish, and Watson completed his hat-trick with an accelerating run that had the crowd on its feet. He finished the scoring by volleying home Yews' centre. It was a seven-goal annihilation of a team who would finish nine places higher in the table, but for seven days Hammers stood at the top of the embryonic Division One. Predictably, they were brought down to earth in their next game, at Aston Villa, when they finished on the wrong end of a 1-6 hiding.

1930-31 was the season West Ham finally put out a new goalkeeper, Bob Dixon. The Hammers' defence leaked 94 goals in just 43 games, their worst ever defensive record in the league to date.

1 Bob Dixon, 2 Alf Earl, 3 Reg Wade, 4 Jimmy Collins, 5 Jim Barrett, 6 Albert Cadwell, 7 Tommy Yews, 8 Stanley Earle (capt), 9 Victor Watson, 10 Billy James, 11 Jimmy Ruffell.

Scorers: Stan Earle 2, 54, Vic Watson 5, 52, 74, 86, Billy James 57
MoM: Jimmy Ruffell
West Ham ended the season: 18th out of 22, with 36 points
(unusual goal-difference: scored 79, conceded 94).

Number: 10	1932-33	Division 2
29th October 1932	Burnley (h)	Att: 12,009

WEST HAM 4 BURNLEY 4

This was the season that took West Ham as near to the Third Division as they'd ever come in their then 48 year history. They've never been as close since. Bizarrely, for a team almost dropping to Division Three, they got to the semi-final of the FA Cup, losing 1-2 to Everton at Molineux. Nearly 50 years later they would again play Everton in an FA Cup semi-final as Second Division underdogs, but this time they would win, going on to beat Arsenal, also from Division One, in the final.

The odd thing about West Ham's exciting tussle with Lancastrian claret and blue crew Burnley in October 1932 was that visiting inside-forward Jones scored all four of their goals, and put the first two into the West Ham net very early in the game without reply. His first came after he advanced into the area after beating two players and hit a powerful shot past George Watson from 25 yards. Just fifteen minutes later he scored a second with another well-taken right-foot shot after the Hammers defence had failed to clear a corner. Hammers managed a swift reply this time when Vic Watson headed in from Fred Norris's corner-kick, and Hammers went in for the half-time break 1-2 down, but still in contention.

In the second half West Ham settled and began to play football academy style, Jackie Morton levelling on 50 minutes after a move involving Mills and Watson. Watson himself finally gave Hammers the lead ten minutes later after a threaded defence-splitting pass from captain Jim Barratt. Unfortunately the lead was short-lived and Burnley's inside-forward line of Hurst, Smith and Jones linked up to provide Jones with his hat-trick six minutes later. They might have been a firm of solicitors, but clearly enjoyed a greater degree of success on the football field. Watson, however, remained the great goalscorer and poacher, and completed his hat-trick to give Hammers the lead again on 70 minutes. Jones spoiled the party but capped a fantastic see-saw game by hammering home a late equaliser for Burnley two minutes from time, his fourth of the game, and more evidence if anyone doubted it, that Upton Park really was the place to go for end-to-end footballing excitement. Victor Watson wore the No 10 shirt just three times that season and this was one of them. It was his only hat-trick that season.

Five months later the two sides met again, this time at Turf Moor, Burnley matching their four goals from the Upton Park game. Hammers, however, were thrashed, scoring a round zero over the 90 minutes, having been tonked 1-6 by neighbours Bury a few weeks earlier. Revenge against that outfit would be another 50 years in coming.

Syd King was suspended by the club for three months on 9th November 1932. Two months later he committed suicide. His method, for the morbidly curious, was to mix a measure of alcohol with a shot of Lysol, the disinfectant of the day. It wasn't the poison that killed him however, according to the post-mortem, it was the bronchial pneumonia that had developed from taking it. He had become depressed since Hammers' relegation and his contract was terminated from the club suddenly following a board meeting on 3rd January 1933 because of growing concerns about his behaviour. Nine days later he was dead.

Flags at the Boleyn Ground were lowered to half-mast, and the whole team donned black armbands for the rest of the season. This was the man who had taken West Ham from the brink of Southern League bankruptcy to Division One status for eight years, with an FA Cup final appearance thrown in. A man who dedicated his life to the club clearly deserved a better end. King may well have been coaching from the 'other side', however, as Hammers won four of their last five games to avoid relegation to the Third Division by a single point.

1 George Watson, 2 Alf Earl, 3 Albert Walker, 4 Bill Johnson, 5 Jim Barrett (capt), 6 Albert Cadwell, 7 Tommy Yews, 8 Fred Norris, 9 Hugh Mills, 10 Victor Watson, 11 Jackie Morton.

Scorers: Victor Watson 42, 60, 70, Jackie Morton 50
MoM: Victor Watson
West Ham ended the season: 20th out of 22, with 35 points
(anotherl crazy goal-difference: scored 75, conceded 93).

Number: 11	1934-35	Division 2
27th April 1935	Bolton (a)	Att: 35,000

BOLTON 3 WEST HAM 1

Bolton Wanderers have often proved to be a bogey side for the Hammers – their opponents in 1923 in their first FA Cup Final (which they lost), the side that beat them in 2003, 80 years later, to deny them Premier League safety in spite of accruing 42 points, a record then for a side getting relegated. Then there was the game in April 1935, twelve years after that cup final, where they needed a win to keep their promotion destiny in their own hands.

This was a thrilling encounter, and a genuine opportunity for the Hammers to get back to the First Division two seasons after avoiding relegation by the shavings of a cat's whisker. Hammers away form was respectable. They had won eight, drawn three and lost nine of their twenty games, but getting something out of this one was still a tall order.

Nevertheless, Hammers made a determined effort to compete in every part of the pitch, matching Bolton across the park in the first half and going close to scoring themselves.

Hammers' goalkeeper Herman Conway was in exceptional form, palming away piledrivers and hurling himself across the goal to keep out headers. However, on twenty minutes following a corner from Walton, Taylor hooked the ball into the net to give Bolton an all-important lead. West Ham knew they couldn't afford to slip further behind and made a determined effort to get back into the match, resulting in an astonishing goal when Len Goulden hit a speculative shot from almost 40 yards that flew past the unprepared Bolton keeper Jones. It was a totally unexpected strike that raised Hammers' hopes and they came close to taking the lead just before half-time after a good move involving Morton and David Mangall.

Bolton came out for the second half as if their lives depended on it, and after just three minutes they restored their lead when Cook found Westwood, who powered in a shot that beat Conway all ends up. When Westwood hit a second eight minutes later, West Ham regrouped with Morton moving to the centre and Mangall to the right wing, but the experiment failed and Hammers struggled to get into the last quarter of the field.

On the hour Mangall, who was struggling with a knock he'd received, couldn't continue, which left the Hammers chasing the game with just ten men. Conway, Chalkley and the captain Barrett all shone in the last twenty minutes, but Bolton had done enough and knew they now carried their fate in their own hands.

On the final day of the season Blackpool held Bolton to a draw which left the Hammers having to beat Oldham by a cricket score, and although they managed two from Barrett and Mangall to win the game, it was never going to be enough in the long run. Bolton went up with Brentford and Hammers would have to fight for one of the two coveted promotion spots another year.

In the final analysis, West Ham had missed out on relegation on goal-average. Even a point at Bolton on that day, as it turned out, would have been enough to send them up to Division One. Instead, they would have to wait another 23 years and the whole of the Second World War before such an opportunity would again come their way.

1 Herman Conway, 2 Alf Chalkley, 3 Albert Walker, 4 Ted Fenton, 5 Jim Barrett (capt), 6 Joe Cockcroft, 7 John Morton, 8 Dr James Marshall, 9 David Mangall, 10 Len Goulden, 11 Jimmy Ruffell.

Scorer: Len Goulden 38
MoM: Herman Conway
West Ham ended the season: 3rd out of 22, with 56 points
(beaten to promotion on goal-average by Bolton, also on 56 points).

Number: 12   1938-39   FA Cup R4 2R
2nd February 1939   Tottenham (Highbury)   Att: 50,648

WEST HAM 2 TOTTENHAM 1

Not unlike the fifth set of a men's tennis match at Wimbledon, where there is no tie-break, FA Cup games in England used to be played replay after replay, extra-time upon extra-time, until a winner was found. So it was in February 1939 with West Ham's FA Cup fixture against arch rivals Tottenham, in the last season before the advent of World War Two.

The fourth round tie between West Ham and Tottenham is probably, with the exception of the 1971-72 League Cup semi-final (games 37 and 38) the most passionate ever fought by a West Ham team. Both sides were then in the top half of the Second Division and with a good chance of featuring in the end-of-season promotion race when they were paired together in the fourth round. Hammers had knocked out QPR 2-1 the round before at Loftus Road, but knew Spurs would be no pushover. They had lost there 1-2 earlier in the season, but the draw sent them to battle at Upton Park. The first game on 21st January was a veritable goal-feast, finishing 3-3, with Hammers' goals from Stan Foxall (2) and Archie Macaulay. The replay at White Hart Lane also finished in a draw, this time 1-1, the Hammers' goal again from Foxall. So, finally, to a second replay, which was played at Highbury before 50,468 spectators caught in a festive atmosphere.

The press captured the zeal of both sets of fans and sent their best reporters out to cover the game. If there had been television coverage, every available station would have been seeking the rights. West Ham started in a more defiant mood, and after Hall had shot straight at Medhurst, Hammers hit Spurs on the break and Sammy Small had a golden opportunity after Morton's cross gave him a clear shot at goal. With only Hooper to beat, Small screwed his shot wide. It was such a good chance that there were murmurings amongst the multitude that he might well regret missing it later.

And that later moment came a little sooner than West Ham would have liked. On the quarter-hour Spurs launched only their second attack of the game when Charlie Walker, instead of leaving the ball to Medhurst, headed it away from the keeper straight into the path of centre-forward Johnny Morrison who, hardly able to believe his luck, hammered the loose ball joyfully into the net. It was another twenty minutes before West Ham began to recover from the shock of falling behind and their striving for an equaliser almost led to a freak goal when Hooper was at full stretch to turn a pass-back from his own player Hall around the post.

In the second half Hammers finally recovered their first-half momentum, bringing Foxall from the right wing into the centre-forward position and pushing Small out to the right. It took over half an hour to come to anything, but when it did the result was well deserved. Macaulay hit a perfectly weighted ball down the middle to Foxall, who accelerated past the defenders and, as Hooper came out, he shot hard and true into the bottom corner of the net, sending Hammers fans into ecstasy. With ten minutes left Hammers looked for a winner in normal time, and first Goulden then Foxall had shots cleared off the line. Sammy Small was having a game he'd rather forget when, in the last minute, Foxall, tightly marked, slipped the ball through to him just six yards out, but with the goal yawning wide open in front of him like a hungry lion, he hit the ball wide. Within a minute the full-time whistle had gone for yet another session of extra time.

West Ham started the extra period well, and after five minutes Foxall's shot hit Spurs' defender Ward in the face with Hooper beaten. This was the only real chance in the first half of extra-time, but just five minutes into the second period Hammers got the goal that would win them the tie. Goulden found Small in his new position out on the right, and his cross was brilliantly dummied by Foxall, leaving Macaulay with the simplest of tap-ins. West Ham were in front for the first time in the whole game!

In the final ten minutes Foxall hit a brilliant shot against the post with Hooper beaten, but West Ham were finally through in this marathon cup-tie after a full five and a half hours of football, and would play Portsmouth nine days later in the fifth round. Unfortunately it was a game that the Hammers lost 0-2, but the joy of beating Spurs in one of the cup-ties of the century was not diminished. Strangely, this was West Ham's last full season in the League until after the Second World War.

As for the FA Cup and replays, the 'penalties' solution to avoid game after game after game only came to the FA Cup in 1991-92, but there are still those who miss the marathon cup-ties of yesteryear from where the expression 'cup tie atmosphere' must surely have originated.

1 Harry Medhurst, 2 Charlie Bicknell (capt), 3 Charlie Walker, 4 Ted Fenton, 5 Dick Walker, 6 Norman Corbett, 7 Stan Foxall, 8 Archie Macaulay, 9 Sammy Small, 10 Len Goulden, 11 John Morton.

Scorers: Stan Foxall 80, Archie Macaulay 110
MoM: Charlie Bicknell
West Ham ended the season: 11th out of 22, with 44 points.

Number: 13	1939-40	League War Cup final
8th June 1940	Blackburn (Wembley)	Att: 42,399

WEST HAM 1 BLACKBURN 0

In a pre-cursor to the Football League Cup, which would be introduced some twenty years later, the Football League War Cup had a two-legged first round. West Ham faced Chelsea, who they beat 3-2 at home before sealing the tie over two legs with an unexpected 2-0 victory at Stamford Bridge.

The Football League had decided in April 1940 to organise a knock-out cup on successive Saturdays with a final projected at Wembley for the second Saturday in June. It was West Ham's first appearance at the great stadium for seventeen years, and they faced Blackburn, who had just been promoted from the Second to the First Division, but who would have to wait seven years until they could take their place in the top flight. With Hammers expecting to follow them into the First Division, the outbreak of war could not have been more untimely. It did mean, however, that there was no clear favourite for the outcome of the game.

Despite being played on a Saturday, the final had a 6.30 evening kick-off, so that factory and general war workers could attend. A crowd of 42,399 was no mean feat in such times. West Ham still employed Charlie Paynter's down the middle tactics to stifle Blackburn's creative wing play, but Blackburn soon reverted to an offside trap. This had Hammers change their approach to working with their wingers to hit crosses at the forwards. Stan Foxall and George Foreman both brought full-length saves from Blackburn keeper James Barron. It was Foxall again, the tricky left-winger, who began the move that was to lead to the only goal of the game. Taking on and beating two Rovers players in the centre-circle, he set off down the left before slipping the ball through to Foreman, whose shot was spilled by Barron directly into the path of the onrunning Sam Small who powered it home. Hammers had failed to beat Blackburn on both opportunities they'd had the previous season, so they knew they had a fight on their hands.

In the second half, both sides threw caution to the wind in an attacking frenzy, but created few genuine opportunities, and with goalkeepers playing well, Hammers' early goal proved to be the only one of the game. In a respite from the troubles of war, the crowd stayed on to see West Ham's captain Charlie Bicknell, once he'd mounted the Wembley steps, receive the cup from Lord Hillsborough. The lap of honour was greeted with great cheers and singing as West Ham could finally get the keys out to that cobweb-covered trophy cabinet at Upton Park.

1939-40 was West Ham's first non-season for over twenty years, the Division Two fixtures abandoned after two Saturdays when war broke out. For the record, Hammers had enjoyed a good start, winning 3-1 away to Plymouth, 2-1 at home to Fulham and going down 0-2 to Leicester, also at home. They were to beat Fulham again narrowly in the Football League War Cup 4-3 in the semi-final, and gained revenge over Leicester by beating them 3-0 at home in a second round replay after a 1-1 draw. The abandoned 1939-40 Division Two season was resurrected in August 1946 using the identical fixtures from those of seven years previously. This time Hammers lost the opener away to Plymouth 1-3, beat Fulham at home 3-2, and again lost at home to Leicester 0-2. The home crowds were improved though, the 13,400 against Leicester in 1939 up to 28,670 in 1946.

1 Herman Conway, 2 Charlie Bicknell (capt), 3 Charlie Walker, 4 Ted Fenton, 5 Dick Walker, 6 Joe Cockcroft, 7 Sammy Small, 8 Archie Macaulay, 9 George Foreman, 10 Len Goulden, 11 Stan Foxall.

Scorer: Sammy Small 34
MoM: Stan Foxall
West Ham ended the season: 2nd in League South 'A,' and 2nd in League South 'C'.

Number: 14	1946-47	Division 2
2nd September 1946	Fulham (h)	Att: 27,900

WEST HAM 3 FULHAM 2

Having imagined they had a side ready to gain promotion to Division One in 1939-40, the onset of World War Two was a cruel blow for the

Hammers. The full extent of that blow was to be seen seven years later when they resumed what they imagined to be another season striving for promotion.

This was one of the three fixtures that had, in a sense, already been played, back in the late summer of 1939 during the aborted fortnight of league football before the Second World War. This, however, from those who were lucky enough to see the previous attempt in August 1939, was a superior game in every respect. It was also West Ham's first post-war league game, attended by nearly 28,000 people.

Fulham, who looked organised and tough, almost scored after just three minutes, Shepherd centering for Buchanan, whose header hit the foot of the post with Medhurst beaten. This gave the west London side confidence, and ten minutes later they took the lead when Woodward dribbled the ball along the goal-line from the corner flag, finding Beasley who slipped in and scored from close range.

Hammers almost had an equaliser when Hinton fumbled a shot from Terry Woodgate and Ed Wood's cross flew across the goal with no one to turn the ball into an empty net. Halfway through the first half, Hinton couldn't hang on to a relatively straightforward centre from Woodgate, and Sammy Small was on the far post to tap it in (this goalkeeping condition was to be repeated in an FA Cup final 29 years later and became known as *Mellorius Fumblius*). Macaulay crashed a shot past Hinton 60 seconds later from the edge of the area following an electrifying move that featured Bicknell, Wood and Woodgate, to put West Ham in front for the first time. Fulham's centre-half Watson had left the field for five minutes with Fulham ahead, and must have been perplexed when he returned from the treatment table to find them a goal down. However this was how the game stayed up until half-time.

The second half was also full of delightful football that kept the crowd entertained, West Ham's fluent and speedy approach play matched by Fulham's more gritty, less subtle but still endearing style of football. This was the beautiful game in peace-time, each set of fans cheering and applauding achievements by both sides in a perversely cordial atmosphere. It was like the sudden rush of empathy you feel for the family of a recently deceased enemy.

Twelve minutes before the end of the game that seemed to have reverted to a gentlemen's knock-about on the village green, West Ham's inside-left Archie Macaulay suddenly ran at the Fulham defence with a burst of acceleration and let fly from the edge of the area with a shot that curled out of Hinton's reach into the top corner. This unexpected goal seemed to stun Fulham into a late burst of action, and Rooke, running on to a loose ball from a hanging Hinton clearance, hit a spectacular cross shot from the edge of the area that perplexed Medhurst. Six minutes from the end Small could have made it four, but his shot bobbled and skimmed off the pitch, hitting the post before bouncing back into play and safely away for a throw.

For twenty minutes or so, time and competitive rivalry subsided in a football ground in London's East End, and 28,000 Londoners remembered the virtues of friendship and shared enjoyment in a ground where such values have often been all too easily forgotten.

1 Harry Medhurst, 2 Charlie Bicknell, 3 Ron Cater, 4 Norman Corbett, 5 Dick Walker (capt), 6 Reg Attwell, 7 Terry Woodgate, 8 George Hall, 9 Sammy Small, 10 Archie Macaulay, 11 Ed Wood.

Scorers: Sammy Small 23, Archie Macaulay 24, 78
MoM: Archie Macaulay
West Ham ended the season: 12th out of 22, with 40 points.

| Number: 15 | 1947-48 | Division 2 |
| 6th March 1948 | Birmingham (a) | Att: 44,000 |

BIRMINGHAM 0 WEST HAM 1

One thing West Ham fans don't need reminding of is their team's peculiar ability to beat anyone on the day, when the conditions are right.

After the war, Birmingham had become the Second Division team everyone wanted to beat. By the beginning of March 1948, they were still unbeaten and sitting proudly at the top of the table in a seemingly unassailable position. Certainly not the best time to have to face them at St Andrews if you were West Ham and having a less than consistent season. Certainly not if you'd just been stuffed 0-2 at home by the other top team of that season, Newcastle.

The only goal of the game came just before half-time when Richard Dunn picked up a through ball from Parsons and as Merrick came out, lifted the ball over him for a perfectly executed goal. The crowd fell silent. Nobody had had the cheek to dare score first against Birmingham for some time.

In the second half West Ham got ten men and the keeper behind the ball, relying on breaks to add to their first-half goal. They only managed a couple in the rest of the game, but when Stephens picked the second of the two second-half chances just five minutes before the end, he should have buried it instead of chipping the ball over the bar. When the final whistle went, all the Birmingham players reacted as if they'd just missed out on promotion by an eighth of a point. In fact they were still five points clear at the top – it was just that their valuable unbeaten record had just been pinched off them by Charlie Paynter's likely lads.

This incredible Birmingham side were managed by Harry Storer, appointed just before the war ended, winning the championship of the 1945–46 Football League (South) wartime league and the Second Division title two years later, despite West Ham spoiling their unbeaten record. They then reached the semi-final of the 1951 FA Cup despite relegation and won promotion again in 1955. The next season Birmingham reached their highest league finish of sixth and their second FA Cup final, and in 1957 reached the semi-finals of the FA Cup and the inaugural Inter-Cities Fairs Cup. That win at St Andrews looks even better put up against all those achievements, but perhaps the Hammers should've gone on to gain that kind of success themselves …

1 Ernie Gregory, 2 Charlie Bicknell, 3 Steve Forde, 4 Norman Corbett, 5 Dick Walker (capt), 6 Tommy Moroney, 7 Terry Woodgate, 8 Eric Parsons, 9 Bill Stephens, 10 Richard Dunn, 11 Don Wade.

Scorers: Richard Dunn 42
MoM: Eric Parsons
West Ham ended the season: 6th out of 22, with 46 points.

| Number: 16 | 1951-52 | FA Cup R3 |
| 12th January 1952 | Blackpool (h) | Att: 38,600 |

WEST HAM 2 BLACKPOOL 1

1951-52 was only Ted Fenton's second year in the manager's hot seat at the Boleyn Ground, Hammer's third manager in over five decades. Only God had been replaced fewer times than West Ham's managers. Apart from the promotion season of 1957-58 and the sixth-place finish in Division One the following season, the FA Cup third round tie against Blackpool in January 1952 was one of Fenton's greatest achievements.

Blackpool was still then described as the 'playground of the North' and looked at as the 'town [which boasted] one of the country's most glamorous and costly football teams' so they didn't anticipate too much grief from an East London Second Division side. They brought down an impressive 2,000 supporters on the day, which boosted the gate to 38,500, a new post-war record. This was the club with 'Donald' the pet duck mascot who was invariably let out of a bag onto the pitch and then re-captured in some kind of bizarre pre-match ritual that seemed to tweak the Lancastrians' funny bones.

Blackpool, apart from possessing the Matthews, Mortensen, Johnston & Co forward line, had been FA Cup finalists in both 1949 and 1951. This line-up was often described as possessing 'probably the world's most expensive forward line'. Ted Fenton hatched what he called 'The F Plan' that he believed could beat Blackpool. He had noticed that Blackpool's right-half could be a little slow on the uptake, so suggested to Ken Tucker, their nifty sprinter left-winger, that he target him for chases down the line.

This was Stanley Matthews' first ever appearance at Upton Park, at a time when one star player could draw neutrals to a game, and they all came to this one. Matthews, in one memorable first-half move, shimmied past Kensell, O'Farrell and Andrews in one continuous weaving body swerve as he took the ball beyond them. Not for nothing had Matthews earned the sobriquet 'The Wizard of the Dribble'. However, when he got anywhere near the West Ham goal, he had Hammers' 20-year-old right-back George Wright to contend with. Wright was a blond-haired, terrier-like ex-Margate defender who didn't know the meaning of the word 'subtle', and he managed to cut out most of Matthews' crosses throughout the game.

After ten minutes, O'Farrell found Tucker, who tricked Shimwell with a Matthews-like swerve, cut inside and pulled the ball back from a position central to the goal-line, Hayward ballooning the cross high into the air. As the ball landed it fell to Jimmy Andrews to volley home with a vengeance.

Incredibly, in the second half West Ham hit a second. Woodgate's corner was cleared to the edge of the area, where O'Farrell promptly hit the loose ball through a crowd of players beyond the unsighted Farm's legs and into the net. The crowd went doodle-eye poppy Country Joe as Blackpool wandered back to the halfway line like a lost netball team in Cheam.

Eight minutes before the end, the Blackpool captain Harry Johnstone, the 1950-51 Footballer of the Year, headed in firmly from Taylor's inswinging corner-kick. It was, however, too little too late, and Hammers were the ones celebrating that evening. Another of their heroes was the man they all called the best uncapped goalkeeper in the country, which he was. That description belonged to one Ernie Gregory who, facing inside forwards Brown and Taylor, amongst others, pulled save after save out of the bag to keep West Ham in the tie.

Most newspapers the next day made it the giant-killing of the competition so far. Hammers, however, always ready to spectacularly disappoint, went out in the next round to Sheffield United, 2-4, after drawing 0-0 at Upton Park.

1 Ernie Gregory, 2 George Wright, 3 Harry Kinsell, 4 Derek Parker, 5 Malcolm Allison (capt), 6 Frank O'Farrell, 7 Terry Woodgate, 8 Gerry Gazzard, 9 Bert Hawkins, 10 Jimmy Andrews, 11 Ken Tucker.

Scorers: Jimmy Andrews 10, Frank O'Farrell 65
MoM: George Wright
West Ham ended the season: 12th out of 22, with 41 points.

Number: 17   1953-54   Division 2
16th January 1954   Fulham (a)   Att: 30,000

FULHAM 3 WEST HAM 4

Back from the dead – as it were. This is an adequate description for this unusual game involving the Hammers, behaving in a very un-Hammers-like fashion. Over the years West Ham have proved on several occasions that the concept of an unassailable lead is flawed (see game 85). Here is one of the very few occasions in their long history when they made their own track marks on that concept.

In the 1953-54 season, West Ham approached the New Year following their typical 'rarely lose at home, never win away' philosophy, which – with the exception of two abberational triumphs at Leeds and Lincoln, had been fulfilled to perfection. Their New Year trip across London to Craven Cottage to face Fulham proved to be the one time they forgot to roll over.

Part of this failure could be put down to the arrival of John Dick for his first season at Upton Park. The freescoring Scot had hit a hat-trick against Bury in November and four other goals going into January, continuing his personal battle with Tommy Dixon, then ahead with eleven in his only full season at the club.

Fulham, however, were promotion candidates that season, difficult to beat on their own ground. This was clear from the first ten minutes of the game as centre-forward Jezzard hit the post with a fierce cross-drive. John Bond kicked the ball off the line following a corner, then captain Malcolm Allison, a little over-exuberant, struck his own post twice with overhit back-passes.

To say Fulham had Hammers on the run would have been an under-statement. Then, as to be expected, Fulham scored. Wing-back Jimmy Hill, gathering a loose ball just outside his own area, ran half the pitch before finding Stevens, who shot past a clump of defenders into the corner of the West Ham net. Just after the half-hour Jezzard took a pass from the great Johnny Haynes, rounded Allison and shot past Gregory from an oblique angle for Fulham's second. Two minutes later Allison, who was in the midst of his own worst personal nightmare, tried to dribble past Haynes in the penalty area, but Haynes intercepted and had the simple task of tapping the ball into an empty net.

Three-nil down with just three minutes of the half remaining. This is when the story starts to take on some far-fetched qualities. A minute later West Ham, in only their second attack of the game, were awarded a free-kick on the edge of the Fulham area. Sexton took it without warning, hitting a crisp shot all along the ground into the corner of the Fulham net. As Fulham kicked off, they lost the ball going forward and Andy Malcolm found John Dick on the halfway line. Dick scampered through to unselfishly lay on a pass to Tommy Dixon for West Ham's second. Fulham could not have been very happy to find themselves only one goal in front after thinking a little earlier that they might have been leading by three.

The second half began as the previous one had ended, and with just 40 seconds played John Dick crashed home an equaliser for the Hammers after Lawler had headed out a corner. Ten minutes later Harry Hooper tied the Fulham defence in a knot with an extended piece of sideways dribbling, then turned and hit a swift pass into the path of John Dick, who struck a powerful shot past Black. For this once, the impossible had been achieved. The Hammers had turned a 0-3 deficit into a 4-3 lead. This they held on to, relatively comfortably it has to be said, for the remaining 30 minutes.

The only other comment to reflect on, perhaps, is that if you check the times, five goals were scored in just eight minutes, a record that would even have Brian Dear smarting.

1 Ernie Gregory, 2 George Wright, 3 Noel Cantwell, 4 Andy Malcolm, 5 Malcolm Allison (capt), 6 Doug Bing, 7 Harry Hooper, 8 Dave Sexton, 9 Tommy Dixon, 10 John Dick, 11 Jimmy Andrews.

Scorers: Dave Sexton 44, Tommy Dixon 45, John Dick 46, 56
MoM: Harry Hooper
West Ham ended the season: 13th out of 22, with 39 points.

Number: 18   1955-56   FA Cup quarter-final
3rd March 1956   Tottenham (a)   Att: 69,111

TOTTENHAM 3 WEST HAM 3

Yet another great cup-tie against Spurs – this one in 1955-56 with West Ham a lower-half Second Division underdog with Spurs in their heyday. Nearly 70,000 spectators crammed into White Hart Lane for this FA Cup quarter-final tie. Hammers had already beaten Preston, Cardiff and Blackburn (away), after a drawn first game at Upton Park.

Memories of Hammers' three-game epic against Spurs in early 1938, some eighteen years earlier, had the Spurs fans looking for revenge. This was clearly ridiculous, as there had been a war and a whole generation of folk passing through the ranks since then, but football fans have long memories, and if a memory can be measured in feet and inches, this one would have been twice the length of a football field.

Billy Dare and John Dick were the Hammers' goal-getters this season, with Harry Hooper (soon to leave for Wolves) and left-winger Ken Tucker. They were all fit and in the starting eleven. It was a sombre and dull afternoon, but the football that was played had something of the height of summer about it.

West Ham more than matched the Spurs side, belying their feeble Second Division position, and there was justice when John Dick put West Ham ahead after a neat move involving the measured passing of Albert Foan. Then Hammers raised the bar and hit a second, Dick again scoring when he beat Reynolds to a high cross from the left by Tucker. It took Spurs a while to settle into their groove, and had Hammers hit a third before they did, then the semi-final place might have been theirs over the 90 minutes.

Tottenham's Smith on the right-wing had taken a knock in the first twenty minutes that had made him something of a passenger for the rest of the game, but Robb began to get the better of his marker John Bond, and rained over a series of crosses that threatened to bring Spurs speedily back into the game. Their reply, when it came, was from the penalty spot, Harmer sending Gregory the wrong way. Dick, however, completed his first half hat-trick three minutes later after a defence-splitting through ball by Hooper. Two minutes on, Spurs had the ball in the net for a second goal, Robb heading in from a corner kick. Five goals had been scored in fifteen minutes, but West Ham were still in the lead.

In the second half, the game lost a little of its momentum, but either of the sides could have added to their tally until the next goal came Spurs' way, Norman bursting through the centre and firing at Gregory who couldn't hold the shot. Harmer gathered the loose ball and found Robb out wide who crossed for Duquemin to head in. West Ham didn't have another goal in them, but nor did Tottenham, and the fact that Hammers were taking them back to Upton Park the following Thursday for a replay seemed victory enough.

The semi-final place evaporated five days later when Spurs played a very different, less open game, stifling West Ham's creativity. Hammers started with the same eleven, but the Saturday fixture had made for heavy legs, and the Division One outfit – in front of an Upton Park capacity crowd of 36,000 – won the game 1-2, Billy Dare scoring the Hammers' goal.

That season's Hammers' squad contained five future First Division managers in Malcolm Allison, John Bond, Noel Cantwell, Dave Sexton and Ken Brown. Hammers won the Southern Floodlight Cup, beating Aldershot 2-1 in the final, played in front of just 5,000 fans, six weeks after the Spurs game. That competition was later renamed the Zenith Data Systems Cup. No, actually joking there.

1 Ernie Gregory, 2 John Bond, 3 Noel Cantwell, 4 Andy Malcolm, 5 Malcolm Allison (capt), 6 Frank O'Farrell, 7 Harry Hooper, 8 Billy Dare, 9 John Dick, 10 Albert Foan, 11 Ken Tucker.

Scorers: John Dick 26, 31, 38
MoM: Harry Hooper
West Ham ended the season: 16th out of 22, with 39 points.

| Number: 19 | 1957-58 | Division 1 |
| 26th April 1958 | Middlesbrough (a) | Att: 30,526 |

MIDDLESBROUGH 1 WEST HAM 3

Malcolm Allison was struck down with tuberculosis in mid-September 1957 during a defeat at promotion contenders Sheffield United that was Hammers' third reverse on the trot. Despite the premature end to the club captain's season, Hammers managed to regroup, winning seven of their next nine fixtures.

In their final home game, a 1-1 draw against fellow promotion chasers Liverpool, it all looked like a possible repeat of the end-of-season disaster of 1934-35. West Ham had also drawn their home game before that, 0-0 against Charlton, and lost 0-1 at Notts County three days afterwards. With only one win in four, Hammers faced their final game at Ayresome Park, home of Middlesbrough. The facts were these: West Ham would return to the First Division as Second Division champions for the first time in 25 years if they won on the last day of 1957-58. Middlesbrough were in 7th position in the league with little to play for except pride, but they had beaten the Hammers in the corresponding fixture the previous season 3-1. Hammers had Dick and Keeble, a goalscoring duo akin to Cottee and McAvennie, each netting 23 goals out of the 101 scored that season.

The big worry for the Hammers was free-scoring Middlesbrough forward Brian Clough, who was streets ahead of any other striker in the division that season with 40 goals and whose incredible career stats read 204 goals in 222 starts. On the day, however, Clough was marked out of the game by the industrious and skilful Ken Brown, giving West Ham the chance to concentrate on the minor matter of getting the ball in the Middlesbrough net.

Hammers took fourteen minutes to score, when John Bond's cross into the area was back-heeled by John Dick past Boro's keeper Peter Taylor. It was a surprisingly modern goal for the times, but typical of the cheeky talent of Hammers' equal top scorer that season. Middlesbrough, however, were playing well, and Arthur Fitzsimons hit an equaliser ten minutes later after Gregory had failed to hold onto Clough's rasping shot. Thankfully Ted Fenton's men hadn't come this far to see their ambitions fade, and five minutes before half-time John Dick provided his fellow goalscorer Vic Keeble with the pass that saw Keeble restore Hammers' lead. Dick made a third for West Ham on the stroke of half-time with a left-footed cross which Malcolm Musgrove put past Taylor for a rare headed goal.

The second half never rose to the excitement of the first as Middlesbrough lost hope, Clough was contained by Brown, and the Hammers knocked the ball about in a shining example of possession football that they would build on the following year in the First Division. Hammers returned to London Kings Cross station later that evening to be met by hoards of fans on an unofficial celebration jaunt. West Ham were back in the First Division. Finally. After 26 years.

Brian Clough's footballing career was cut short by an injury after his move to Sunderland, but he teamed up with Middlesbrough keeper and teammate Peter Taylor to take first Derby County and then Nottingham Forest to a series of First Division championships and European Cup victories.

1 Ernie Gregory, 2 John Bond, 3 Noel Cantwell (capt), 4 Andy Malcolm, 5 Ken Brown, 6 Andy Nelson, 7 Mike Grice, 8 John Smith, 9 Vic Keeble, 10 John Dick, 11 Malcolm Musgrove.

Scorers: John Dick 14, Vic Keeble 40, Malcolm Musgrove 45
MoM: Ken Brown
West Ham ended the season: 1st out of 22, with 57 points
(promoted – ahead of rivals Blackburn by a single point).

Number: 20	1958-59	Division 1
8th September 1958	Manchester United (h)	Att: 35,672

WEST HAM 3 MANCHESTER UNITED 2

Billy Lansdowne had suffered a bad knock in West Ham's first defeat of the season, a 1-4 pounding at the hands of Luton, two days earlier, so manager Ted Fenton was faced with a dilemma. Hammers' opponents on the Monday night, Manchester United, had just thumped Blackburn Rovers 6-1, so playing a half fit Lansdowne was a risky strategy in an age when there were no substitutes in football. Recovering from tuberculosis after a long year was the manager's natural choice, Malcolm Allison, who had played a major part in the team's development over the last few seasons, and who was desperate to get back into the first team after his long lay-off to enjoy the First Division football his talent and previous efforts clearly deserved.

However, Allison had lost a lung in his extended convalescence from tuberculosis, and despite the fact that he had spent much of that time taking coaching sessions with the Hammers' youngsters, improving his natural fitness, he was still a big risk. The legend goes that, unable to make the decision, Fenton turned to his club captain Noel Cantwell for an opinion. Cantwell suggested Fenton look to the 17-year-old youngster at the club who had already been capped for his country at youth level, Robert Moore. It proved an excellent suggestion, and thankfully Fenton took it.

The goalscoring machine that was John Dick took just seven minutes to get off the mark in the match, chasing Bond's long ball through on the left before firing home a perfectly measured shot past Harry Gregg. United's McGuiness painfully pulled a thigh muscle a few minutes later, but limped on, Busby having to reorganise his side to stop West Ham getting on top. The reshuffled side struggled, however, and just before half-time a neat flick from Keeble after Dick's pass set Smith up with a scoring chance which he took, firing in from twenty yards past Gregg. A two-goal cushion at half-time meant Hammers could look optimistically to going top of the table that night with nine points from their first six games.

The second half, however, was a very different story. Busby's half-time team talks were legendary, and United began well after the restart with Charlton and Violett both coming close, but it was the Hammers who went 3-0 up on the hour, Musgrove collecting the ball from a poor clearance and rifling his shot through a crowd of players to send the 35,000 crowd into a frenzy.

This excitement seemed to strangely raise United's spirits, and those of the struggling Wilf McGuiness, who made United's first goal nine minutes later with a left-footed cross to the far post, where Colin Webster headed home past Ernie Gregory. Not happy with making one, McGuiness then contrived to score a second for United, hitting a cross shot from twenty yards over Gregory as he advanced down the left wing. United were denied an equaliser when Freddie Goodwin headed over from just in front of the six-yard box, but the Hammers held on to take the points in what all the journalists present agreed was a genuine one-off that Monday evening.

Bobby Moore made the first of five appearances in the first team that season, and drew enthusiastic plaudits from the Manchester United manager Matt Busby. The victory took West Ham to the top of the First Division with four wins from the first six games. And then, guess what? Hammers were turned over 0-4 at Nottingham Forest and 1-4 at Old Trafford – swift revenge for the Busby Babes. Yet more proof of misery emerging from joy for Hammers' fans, if any were needed. Hammers recovered later in the season, and the following year Bobby Moore emerged again to finally claim the No 6 jersey for himself, a number he would come to make his own in every team he played for in the career years to come.

Club captain Malcolm Allison, however, never recovered to full fitness from losing a lung to tuberculosis, and did not play again for the Hammers.

1 Ernie Gregory, 2 John Bond, 3 Noel Cantwell (capt), 4 Andy Malcolm, 5 Ken Brown, 6 Bobby Moore, 7 Mike Grice, 8 John Smith, 9 Vic Keeble, 10 John Dick, 11 Malcolm Musgrove.

Scorers: John Dick 8, John Smith 36, Malcolm Musgrove 59
MoM: Andy Malcolm
West Ham ended the season: 6th out of 22, with 48 points (equalling their then best ever league position).

Number: 21   1958-59   Division 1
31st January 1959   Nottingham Forest (h)   Att: 26,676

WEST HAM 5 NOTTINGHAM FOREST 3

In West Ham's first season in the First Division following their promotion year, this was probably the game and the performance of the campaign. Any of the eight goals scored was a contender for goal of the season, had there been cameras at Upton Park to witness them.

Forest were mid-table, but rarely drew their away games, their attacking style tending to be rewarded with victories or heavy defeats. They were one of the most exciting teams in the First Division. With Hammers also playing attacking football under Ted Fenton, this was a game to attract the neutrals as well as the Forest and West Ham fans.

Forest came out on the attack, as if they were playing at home, with four men up front. One, Johnny Quigley, a speedy inside-forward who would feature prominently in Forest's FA Cup final win over Luton Town later in the year, escaped from the Hammers' defence after ten minutes to give Forest an early lead. John Dick, who would gain his only Scottish international cap against England that summer, equalised eight minutes later from new-boy Woosnam's pass, his right-foot shot flashing past Thomson before the Forest goalie could move.

Dick did it again ten minutes later, again with his weaker right foot, to give Hammers the lead, though this time he was on the turn, his back to the keeper, to volley home. One of Dick's talents was an uncanny awareness of where the goal was at all times; he might well have made an excellent goalkeeper for that very reason. Forest equalised seven minutes later in this see-saw game when Tommy Wilson got up to head Stewart Imlach's cross past Ernie Gregory. Forest were without their manager Billy Walker, who had gone down with a chill, but were certainly worth a share of the spoils up to half-time when the teams went in for the break two apiece.

Phil Woosnam hit a typical dipping volley on the hour after collecting Brown's pass from Gregory's clearance, but then came the goal of the game, and it was scored by Forest. Roy Dwight, gathering a loose ball out of defence, ran two thirds the length of the field. It took him past Ken Brown, Andy Malcolm, captain Noel Cantwell, and finally the keeper Gregory before he filed the ball into the corner of the net to make the score 3-3. Dwight's genius was reflected in his 27 goals for Forest in just 53 appearances. He was also the uncle of a certain Reg Dwight, better known subsequently as Elton John.

West Ham had been pinned back twice, but this was the time they stepped up a gear to take the game out of Forest's reach. Vic Keeble who, like Dick, had already scored fourteen goals coming into this match, hit a brace in the last twenty minutes. Two minutes after Dwight's solo effort, Keeble struck a beauty on the volley from a cross from the right wing and then, five minutes from time, roared through the middle after Andy Malcolm's through ball and whacked it past Charlie 'Chic' Thomson – twenty years before the poor dance-loving man would have a decent double meaning for his nickname.

It was a fantastic season for the Hammers in their first year back after promotion, and they finally finished it in sixth position, the second best placing in their history. It was also the final campaign for many of the older players as manager Ted Fenton began to bring in new blood to endeavour to make Hammers a real force in the First Division in the 1960s.

1 Ernie Gregory, 2 John Bond, 3 Noel Cantwell (capt), 4 Andy Malcolm, 5 Ken Brown, 6 John Smith, 7 Harry Grice, 8 Phil Woosnam, 9 Vic Keeble, 10 John Dick, 11 Malcolm Musgrove.

Scorers: John Dick 18, 29, Phil Woosnam 62, Vic Keeble 70, 84
MoM: Phil Woosnam
West Ham ended the season: 6th out of 22, with 48 points.

| Number: 22 | 1960-61 | Division 1 |
| 5th November 1960 | Arsenal (h) | Att: 29,375 |

WEST HAM 6 ARSENAL 0

David Dunmore isn't a household name even in the most ardent of West Ham supporting households, but on 5th November 1960 the Yorkshire striker achieved something remarkable in terms of Hammers' history: a hat-trick against Arsenal. At that point, however, Arsenal had not beaten West Ham since World War Two, a pleasure that was to be continually denied them until March 1963.

Arsenal's manager George Swindin hadn't enjoyed the greatest of successes with his mid-table Arsenal outfit, but this result was never on the cards with both sides in similar league form. However, just four minutes had elapsed when Dunmore was gifted a goal after a dreadful error by Billy McCullough. On the half-hour he hit a second after a great move involving Woosnam and a delicate touch from John Dick, leaving West Ham two ahead at the interval.

The second half started with the Hammers continuing with manager Ted Fenton's 4-2-4 formation, Woosnam and Moore playing behind the strikers. Welsh wizard Woosnam was on top form with his mazy runs and dizzy dribbling to confound the weary Arsenal defence. For all their domination, however, the game may have finished up a regulation West Ham victory until – in a crazy nineteen-minute spell, they finally blew Arsenal away.

The third goal came from John Dick, set up by Grice, who rounded Wills and Kelsey before laying the ball across goal to Dick at the far post. Eight minutes later Woosnam, man of the match, poached one for himself from just inside the area. The fifth was the only First Division goal Andy Malcolm ever scored in his career, a fine touch from a corner by Derek Woodley, and Dunmore wrapped up the 6-0 annihilation in the last minute after being put through by Woosnam to complete his hat-trick.

Their victory set Hammers on a fine five-match run, winning three and scoring sixteen goals, the last ten of which came in a 5-5 draw at Newcastle and a 5-0 thrashing of Wolves. The second half of the season, however, was dire, and Hammers finally slumped to sixteenth, just four points above relegated Newcastle.

1 Brian Rhodes, 2 John Bond, 3 John Lyall, 4 Andy Malcolm, 5 Ken Brown, 6 Bobby Moore, 7 Derek Woodley, 8 Phil Woosnam (capt), 9 David Dunmore, 10 John Dick, 11 Harry Grice.

Scorers: Dunmore 4, 32, 89, Dick 70, Woosnam 78, Malcolm 83
MoM: Phil Woosnam
West Ham ended the season: 16th out of 22, with 36 points.

Number: 23	1961-62	Division 1
16th December 1961	Manchester United (a)	Att: 29,472

MANCHESTER UNITED 1 WEST HAM 2

There can't have been many top division meetings between West Ham and Manchester United when West Ham were fourth in the table and United 20th, but this was a season when Hammers, with the two veterans John Dick and Malcolm Musgrove scoring goals for fun, were a team to be feared at Upton Park and on the road.

Bobby Moore had just returned from suspension for his sending off against Manchester City the previous month, and gave a typically composed performance to organise his defence and help West Ham gain another vital away win to keep them in the top four.

United were a desperate team, still rebuilding and recovering from the Munich disaster, but they gave all they'd got in an entertaining and frantic game played under floodlights on a dark and gloomy Saturday afternoon. Hammers' record at Old Trafford was utter pants: a 1-4 reverse followed by a 3-5 and a 1-6. But this was an afternoon when they were not to be roasted, despite the Saturday pundits' unanimous predictions that they would be.

Hammers began well, and had the ball in the back of the net after eleven minutes, only for a linesman's flag to rule Woosnam's effort offside. Incredibly, United took this as a prompt to galvanise themselves into action and David Herd slipped in between two defenders to force home an opener past Leslie. Whilst conceding a goal against the run of play has traditionally been a cue for Hammers to fold, this goal inspired a calm and concentrated approach to the rest of the half. Woosnam at the centre, sprayed passes to Crawford and Musgrove and set up chances for Dick and Tindall that on any other day might have seen the Hammers two or three up by half-time. As it was, United's keeper David Gaskell kept the Irons at bay, preserving United's slender lead. Lawrie Leslie, too, was no spectator, being forced to make two brilliant saves in succession from Lawton and Bobby Charlton.

Manager Ron Greenwood, in his first full season at the club, told his side to be patient and continue with the way they were playing, which was what happened in the second half as Hammers gradually took control. The equaliser didn't come until a quarter of an hour from time, but it was from the trusty left foot of Scottish striker John Dick, hitting his fifteenth goal of the season, his sixteenth coming ten minutes later to give Hammers the lead they had been courting for some time.

The margin flattered United at the end, but it was a testimony to the Hammers' control that they knew they had done enough, and were rarely threatened in the last part of the game. One match and one more win later, Hammers went second in the First Division, only to fall away in the second half of the season, ending up eighth. Nevertheless, the win at Old Trafford inspired a revival in the Manchester side, helping them to finish 15th after seeming certainties for relegation at Christmas.

John 'Jackie' Dick ended his career at West Ham with 166 goals in 351 games, finishing the third highest goalscorer for the club behind Geoff Hurst and the legendary Vic Watson.

1 Lawrie Leslie, 2 Joe Kirkup, 3 John Bond, 4 Geoff Hurst, 5 Ken Brown, 6 Bobby Moore, 7 Ian Crawford, 8 Phil Woosnam (capt), 9 Ron Tindall, 10 John Dick, 11 Malcolm Musgrove.

Scorers: John Dick 75, 85
MoM: John Dick
West Ham ended the season: 8th out of 22, with 44 points.

Number: 24	1962-63	Division 1
8th September 1962	Manchester City (a)	Att: 25,000

MANCHESTER CITY 1 WEST HAM 6

This was Ron Greenwood's second full season at Upton Park, and he was well into his master plan to turn the side into the greatest attacking proponents of total football that the country had ever seen. The latest part of the reshaping had seen the departure of John Dick, two days before this game, for £17,500. Dick had been at the club for nine seasons, and his departure to Brentford, then of the Fourth Division, was a record for the club and the division. Greenwood used some of that money to buy the talented Peter Brabrook from Chelsea for £35,000. He joined Johnny 'Budgie' Byrne in the front line, signed from Crystal Palace in March for a record-breaking £65,000.

West Ham faced a City side propping up the First Division, and with the Hammers in 19th place themselves, just three positions higher, it didn't look like a pretty match on paper. In their first six league games, Hammers had only scored four goals. That total would be more than doubled in the ensuing 90 minutes.

Malcolm Musgrove put the Hammers ahead after 27 minutes from just inside the area, but City were level within a minute through Colin Barlow. This was to be City's only moment of success in the whole game. Hammers restored their lead ten minutes later through Tony Scott, his second in two games, having scored the only goal against Liverpool the previous Monday. Three minutes later Hammers netted a third through the free-scoring 'Budgie' Byrne, and after another three minutes Martin Peters had made it 4-1, after playing a typical one-two with Hurst. For a team which had only won one of their first six matches, a 4-1 half-time lead away from home was an unexpected luxury.

After 25 minutes of the second half, and no further goals, the most extraordinary event occurred. Convinced that Tony Scott was offside on the break, the whole City defence stopped, only for Malcolm Musgrove to continue into the area and head in Scott's cross to give West Ham a fifth. Veteran goalkeeper Bert Trautmann was so irate with the officials that he ran half the pitch in pursuit of the referee, and after heated words picked up the ball and blasted it into the referee's back from point-blank range. Anticipating the official's response, the German keeper, blond locks flowing, removed his goalkeeping jersey and threw it to the ground before leaving the field.

West Ham's final goal was scored by Geoff Hurst in the 80th minute, his first of the season and only his second ever for the club. Hurst had originally been played as a wing-half by Ron Greenwood, but this was the season when Greenwood finally switched him to an out-and-out striker. He then scored fifteen goals in his next 27 appearances, earning himself for the first time the achievement of being top scorer. This game was only his second after being switched from the No 4 shirt to the No 10 that would become his career number. Within four years he would become the first and only man to score a hat-trick in a World Cup final.

The same fixture the previous season had seen Bobby Moore sent off for the firsst and last time in his career, so the 6-1 win was a particularly satisfying result for the newly elected West Ham captain and his team.

1 Lawrie Leslie, 2 John Bond, 3 Jackie Burkett, 4 Martin Peters, 5 Ken Brown, 6 Bobby Moore (capt), 7 Tony Scott, 8 Phil Woosnam, 9 Johnny Byrne, 10 Geoff Hurst, 11 Malcolm Musgrove.

Scorers: Musgrove 27, 70, Scott 37, Byrne 40, Peters 43, Hurst 80
MoM: Tony Scott
West Ham ended the season: 12th out of 22, with 40 points.

Number: 25	1963-64	Division 1
14th September 1963	Liverpool (a)	Att: 45,495

LIVERPOOL 1 WEST HAM 2

This was Liverpool's second season in the First Division after their pro-motion in 1961-62, but Bill Shankly had already built a reputation as their dour, dry-humoured Scottish manager, taking them to eighth in his first top-flight season with them, and masterminding their FA Cup quarter-final victory over the Hammers at Anfield with a Roger Hunt goal, nine minutes from time. With Liverpool also having won at Anfield in the league, West Ham were hoping their next visit, early in 1963-64, might prove third time lucky, and this time they were right.

This game saw the debut of Dave Bickles, who was to make only two further appearances for the Hammers that season, but still picked a good match to call his first for West Ham. At centre-half that day he took on and marked out of the game the irrepressible Scottish striker Ian St John. Hammers had begun the season with two wins, two draws and two defeats, and stood ninth. Liverpool were eleventh, having lost their first two home games, so Hammers were favourites to get a result, as they were unbeaten on the road.

West Ham were first out of the traps, playing a more attacking game than in their previous away fixture, which they had won 1-0 at Blackpool with a penalty from 'Budgie' Byrne. They took the lead eleven minutes into the game, when Peters slotted the ball home expertly after Bobby Moore's side-splitting through ball. Geoff Hurst added a second ten minutes later with a coolly finished lob over Jim Furnell. With few chances falling to either side, a two-goal lead looked to be enough for the whole game and it got Hammers to half-time feeling pretty confident of bagging both points.

In the second half, the Anfield crowd made the kind of noise for which they would become famous, and lifted their side to begin to play the kind of football that had already given them such a reputation. On the hour, Bobby Moore handled and Ronnie Moran prepared to put Liverpool back into contention. In front of the kop, however, Jim Standen made a fantastic save to preserve Hammers' two-goal lead. Not for long. For the second season in a row Roger Hunt netted against the Hammers. He beat three players, including Bobby Moore, before poking the ball past Standen. With 25 minutes left, Liverpool hoped to snatch their first home point of the season but Hammers held out to record their second successive league away win.

Bizarrely, West Ham have not won at Anfield since. Interestingly enough, it was the last time Liverpool were to lose at home that season. The second half of their campaign would see a burst of form which would take them top of the league, and by the end of 1963-64 the Reds would celebrate their first League championship under Bill Shankly. They would claim it again in 1966 and many more times in the decades to come.

1 Jim Standen, 2 Joe Kirkup, 3 Jackie Burkett, 4 Martin Peters, 5 Dave Bickles, 6 Bobby Moore (capt), 7 Peter Brabrook, 8 Ronnie Boyce, 9 Johnny Byrne, 10 Geoff Hurst, 11 Brian Dear.

Scorers: Martin Peters 11, Geoff Hurst 34
MoM: Martin Peters
West Ham ended the season: 14th out of 22, with 40 points.

| Number: 26 | 1963-64 | FA Cup final |
| 2nd May 1964 | Preston (Wembley) | Att: 100,000 |

WEST HAM 3 PRESTON 2

West Ham's sixth season back in the First Division, and Ron Greenwood's third since taking over, saw Hammers drop another couple of positions to 14th by May 1964, which might have raised questions about his achievements, had it not been for West Ham reaching their second FA Cup final and their first for 41 years. They had also reached their first League Cup semi-final, but were knocked out by Leicester, thanks to the brilliance of England goalkeeper Gordon Banks. Banks would deny West Ham in the same competition at the same stage for Stoke City eight years later.

West Ham had done the hard work in the FA Cup semi-final, beating Manchester United 3-1 at Hillsborough, and now faced Second Division Preston in the final for their first domestic trophy since the FA War Cup in 1940. Would it be an easy game? The Hammers had suffered a record home defeat that season, 2-8, to Blackburn on Boxing Day 1963, so were capable of falling apart to virtually anyone. 'Budgie' Byrne and Bobby Moore were left out of the Hammers' final league game, at home to Everton, so they could go and 'spy' on Preston. Hammers lost 0-2, and in fact lost four of their last five in the league. All that mattered now was getting that first ever FA Cup to parade.

Moore had four days earlier been named Footballer of the Year by the Football Writers Association, so it was with double pride that he led his side out at Wembley. Both sides fielded the obligatory teenager: West Ham had eighteen-year-old John Sissons, while Preston gave a game to seventeen-year-old Howard Kendall, the youngest player to feature in a Wembley final.

Preston, unfortunately for the Hammers, played the game of their lives. Despite being a Second Division team, they attacked from the start and deservedly opened the scoring after ten minutes. From West Ham's point of view, it was a dreadful goal to concede. Dawson's bobbling shot was pushed out by Standen into the path of Holden, who tapped it in at the far post.

Thankfully West Ham were soon level, young Sissons firing home with his left foot from just inside the Preston area. Yet Preston continued to lay siege to the Hammers' goal, Dawson restoring their lead five minutes before half-time with a firm header from Wilson's hanging corner. It wasn't the half-time score that most expected.

In the second half, Hammers continued to keep Preston at bay, whilst taking every effort to hit their opponents on the break. Their equaliser, when it came on 52 minutes, was fortuitous. Peter Brabrook's outswinging corner was headed by Ken Brown towards goal, where Geoff Hurst headed the ball towards the top corner. The ball hit the underside of the bar (the other end of the pitch to where he would score his second World Cup goal two years later), and was helped over the line by Preston keeper Alan Kelly as he tried to pull the ball to safety. These days it would go down as an own-goal, but Hurst's claims were honoured, and West Ham were level.

The next 35 minutes provided end-to-end entertainment as Hammers and Preston both looked for the goal that might win the game. Both sides were tiring in the final minutes, ready for extra-time, but West Ham had just one more trick up their sleeves. A low cross from the right from Hurst, socks round his ankles, was headed goalwards by Ronnie Boyce, running in, who saw his effort drop into the corner of the net for a last-minute winner.

This was Bobby Moore's finest moment to date – the Footballer of the Year lifting the FA Cup from the Wembley steps to celebrate West Ham's finest achievement to date – though there was more to come in the next twelve months!

On the Monday before the final, Preston had sent an eleven down to provide opposition for John Lyall's testimonial. The young Hammer had been forced to retire from playing prematurely as a result of a leg injury, and 18,000 fans turned up to wish him well.

Lyall would soon be back at the club, on his way up the greasy managerial pole, eventually to guide West Ham to their highest ever league position.

1 Jim Standen, 2 John Bond, 3 Jackie Burkett, 4 Eddie Bovington, 5 Ken Brown, 6 Bobby Moore (capt), 7 Peter Brabrook, 8 Ronnie Boyce, 9 Johnny Byrne, 10 Geoff Hurst, 11 John Sissons.

Scorers: John Sissons 12, Geoff Hurst 52, Ronnie Boyce 90
MoM: Ronnie Boyce
West Ham ended the season: 14th out of 22, with 40 points.

Number: 27   1964-65   ECWC final
19th May 1965   TSV Munich 1860 (Wembley)   Att: 100,000

WEST HAM 2 TSV MUNICH 1860 0

West Ham's first ever FA Cup win occurred in the early days of automatic qualification for European competition, but English clubs were novices and had yet to assert themselves consistently, although Tottenham had won the Cup-Winners' Cup two years earlier. Little was expected from the Hammers, already legendary for their league inconsistency but, as they have often proved, cups provided challenges they could rise to.

Hammers had drawn with Liverpool 2-2 at the start of the season to share the Charity Shield, played at Anfield as opposed to Wembley. As with the previous season, Ron Greenwood introduced no new players of note. His side usually played well at home and poorly away. In Europe, however, West Ham were only beaten once on the road throughout the competition, losing 1-2 at Czechoslovak Cup-holders Spartak Prague, after two late goals. West Ham still went through 3-2 on aggregate, thanks to a 2-0 first leg win at Upton Park.

West Ham's good fortune was that the final had been allocated at the outset to Wembley, so when Hammers held Spanish side Real Zaragoza 1-1 away in the semi-final second leg, having enjoyed a 2-1 home advantage, they knew they would be at Wembley again, this time to face the German side TSV Munich 1860.

Winning five of their final eight league games, Hammers finished ninth in the First Division, so were in form when they ran out to face their West German opponents. Brian Dear had retained his place, thanks to his five-goal haul against West Brom the previous month, and Alan Sealey was in for the absent 'Budgie' Byrne, West Ham's top scorer that season with 29 goals.

It was an exciting final, both sides playing attacking football but moving cautiously out of defence. Hammers had the edge going forward, Sissons hitting the post early on, and Dear getting into good positions for Moore's aerial passes across the Wembley turf. 'Stag' even had a 'goal' disallowed for offside on the half-hour. Greenwood, as always, had done his homework and organised a marking system on the German danger-men, who rarely bothered Standen in the first half. At the other end, Yugoslavian international keeper Peter Radenkovic was kept busy, but proved himself adept at handling whatever was thrown at him.

West Ham continued to press in the second half. They got their reward in the 69th minute when Alan Sealey, driven wide to reach a cross from Ronnie Boyce, hit a ferocious angled shot between the keeper and the near post. Two minutes later Sealey was on hand again, this time to poke in the loose ball after Peters had failed to bring Moore's cross under control. The crowd, still celebrating the first goal, roared even louder. Hammers might have had more when Sissons hit the bar, but the Germans, who had performed well, had little extra to give and Bobby Moore was soon climbing the Wembley steps for the second successive season. He lifted the European Cup-Winners' Cup, still by a long chalk the greatest single achievement by a West Ham team.

Moore would collect a losers' medal for Fulham ten years later in the 1975 FA Cup final, but his greatest Wembley achievement was, though he didn't know it then, just over a year away, when he would lift the Jules Rimet World Cup trophy.

1 Jim Standen, 2 Joe Kirkup, 3 Jackie Burkett, 4 Martin Peters, 5 Ken Brown, 6 Bobby Moore (capt), 7 Alan Sealey, 8 Ronnie Boyce, 9 Geoff Hurst, 10 Brian Dear, 11 John Sissons.

Scorers: Alan Sealey 69, 71
MoM: Bobby Moore
West Ham ended the season: 9th out of 22, with 42 points.

Number: 28	1966-67	Division 1
17th December 1966	Chelsea (a)	Att: 47,805

CHELSEA 5 WEST HAM 5

West Ham have often provided entertainment when travelling across London to face west London's finest, Chelsea, and in December 1966 they shared ten goals in a game still referred to by those that saw it as the most exciting London derby ever in the top flight.

West Ham have enjoyed some great victories at Stamford Bridge over the years, but when they took a two-goal lead through Peter Brabrook and Martin Peters it looked like avenging a 2-6 tonking suffered at the Bridge the previous season.

Chelsea were second in the table, despite having won just three games at home. Brabrook cut inside two Chelsea defenders to place the ball past Bonetti for West Ham's first. Peters scored the second from a corner five minutes later. Hammers had lost to Chelsea 1-2 on the opening day of the season, which was their first league game after England's World Cup triumph, and when Tommy Baldwin reduced the arrears after a mix up between Bovington and Charles, it meant West Ham held the narrowest of leads as the teams went off at half-time.

Perhaps there was something in the Chelsea players' tea at the break, as they hit two in three minutes after the restart to take the lead. Hateley beat Moore in the air to head the equaliser, and Charlie Cooke then walloped a volley past Standen.

Incredibly, West Ham then hit three of their own in the following five minutes. John Sissons scored two in two to restore West Ham's lead. Both goals stemmed from breaks down the left, from where Sissons scored with his left foot.

On both occasions Ron 'Chopper' Harris intervened too late even to make contact with the nippy winger. On the hour West Ham were awarded a penalty to make it 5-3, but Peter Bonetti saved it – 'Budgie' Byrne's second ever miss for the Hammers. However, the rebound fell for Byrne to net with relief.

With ten minutes to go, West Ham's two-goal lead looked unassailable but the match took a final twist that had one reporter referring to it as an 'Alfred Hitchcock type thriller'. Moore, who had struggled with the antics of Tony Hateley throughout the game, brought him down in the 81st minute, and Bobby Tambling stroked home the penalty. Two minutes into injury-time Chelsea had their reward when Tambling scored his second to bring Chelsea level again.

This game remains the highest scoring draw in the Football League history, probably because if your team is good enough to score five, then it's unlikely to be feeble enough to concede five (unless you support either of these sides).

West Ham had been involved in another 5-5 draw away from home, at Newcastle in December 1960, and on that occasion they led 5-2 with eleven minutes left. Don't ever say West Ham can't play the charity outfit when they want!

1 Jim Standen, 2 Eddie Bovington, 3 John Charles, 4 Martin Peters, 5 Ken Brown, 6 Bobby Moore (capt), 7 Peter Brabrook, 8 Ron Boyce, 9 Johnny Byrne, 10 Geoff Hurst, 11 John Sissons, 12 Dennis Burnett.

Scorers: Brabrook 24, Peters 29, Sissons 55, 58, Byrne 60p
MoM: John Sissons
West Ham ended the season: 16th out of 22, with 36 points.

Number: 29   1967-68   Division 1
8th September 1967   Sunderland (a)   Att: 39,772

SUNDERLAND 1 WEST HAM 5

Any Hammers fan will tell you that, traditionally, West Ham rarely score more than two goals per game away from home, but in this match in September 1967, following the summer of love, Hammers hit five. They were facing a side unbeaten at home, nine places higher in the league, and went there having conceded eighteen goals in their first six games. A further odd fact is that West Ham trailed 0-1 at half-time, Bobby Moore turning Scottish international Neil Martin's cross past Jim Standen.

The second half saw West Ham at their on-the-road best, but even so, nothing remarkable happened until the last half hour. Martin Peters put West Ham level with a 25-yard piledriver into the roof of the net. Sixty seconds later Geoff Hurst headed West Ham into the lead from a Brooking cross. Two minutes after that Redknapp fired from 30 yards over Montgomery into the back of the net.

West Ham had gone from trailing to 3-1 up in a little over four minutes, and there was still more to come. Hurst tapped in a fourth, following a three-man move with Brabrook and Boyce. The final goal was struck by Moore from 30 yards, fifteen minutes from time. Hammers had scored five in fifteen minutes and Sunderland were stunned. By the time the final whistle went, there were probably more West Ham fans in the ground than home fans.

But it was that kind of season. A month later Hammers squandered a three-goal half-time lead over Stoke to end up losing 3-4. In February they thrashed Fulham 7-2 and in March hit Newcastle 5-0, with Trevor Brooking scoring a hat-trick in his first season at the club.

1 Jim Standen, 2 John Charles, 3 Bill Kitchener, 4 Martin Peters, 5 John Cushley, 6 Bobby Moore (capt), 7 Harry Redknapp, 8 Trevor Brooking, 9 Geoff Hurst, 10 Ronnie Boyce, 11 Peter Brabrook, 12 Peter Bennett.

Scorers: Peters 60, Hurst 61, 75, Redknapp 63, Moore 76
MoM: Bobby Moore
West Ham ended the season: 12th out of 22, with 38 points.

Number: 30   1968-69   Division 1
19th October 1968   Sunderland (h)   Att: 24,718

WEST HAM 8 SUNDERLAND 0

Brian Dear had scored five against West Brom in just twenty minutes four seasons earlier. Hurst's tally against Sunderland took a little longer, but was no less impressive.

What makes a high-scoring game like this? Why would a player score six goals in a game – effectively a double hat-trick – just once in his career? And why *this* game?

For all the great goalscoring footballers in history, only one has ever scored a hat-trick in a World Cup final. He is also one of two footballers to score six in one game for West Ham. The other was Vic Watson against Leeds at Upton Park on 9th February 1929, when West Ham also scored eight, Leeds scoring two in reply. It took nearly 40 years before that achievement was emulated by Geoff Hurst.

It was the fourteenth time West Ham had played Sunderland at Upton Park. They had only beaten the Black Cats twice in the league in thirteen games, and once in the FA Cup, in 1929. There was nothing in the records to hint at the mauling that Sunderland were to suffer, especially as the Hammers hadn't won at home for two months. They had also experienced only their second player ever to be sent off under Ron Greenwood, this being a young Harry Redknapp for backchatting the referee after a retaliatory foul on Billy Bremner. This proves that very special matches often arrive unannounced.

Redknapp should have opened the scoring in the first minute, when he got behind the Sunderland defence but put the ball wide. Even in this high-scoring fiesta, it took eighteen minutes before West Ham opened their account, when Hurst dived low to head home Martin Peters' cross. At least he *appeared* to head the ball; Hurst admitted afterwards that the ball had gone in off his hand. So his account was opened somewhat fortuitously. No debate about the second, though, as Bobby Moore hit a free-kick from 35 yards past the stationary Montgomery. Ten minutes later Billy Bonds found Brooking, who crossed for Hurst to head home his second at the far post. West Ham's fourth came a minute before half-time when Bonds found Redknapp from a corner, and the subsequent cross was hit first time by Hurst into the net to give him a half-time hat-trick. It was Hurst's first hat-trick for a year.

The second half was no less frenetic. Peters found Hurst three minutes after the break. Hurst chested the ball down before firing it into the net. He equalled Dear's West Brom tally with a fifth from 25 yards, which may have enjoyed a deflection or two before it found its way past Montgomery. Brooking got on the scoresheet with an angled shot as he bore down on goal. Hurst's double hat-trick, from which he might have claimed a couple of balls to take home, came just over a quarter of an hour from time, after a low cross from Redknapp evaded everyone but the big man.

Strangely, the match was watched by West Ham's lowest crowd of the season. Despite there being no more goals, few left the ground in case they missed West Ham's biggest victory ever. In that 8-0 trouncing, there were no goals scored in the first or last quarters of an hour.

1 Bobby Ferguson, 2 Billy Bonds, 3 John Charles, 4 Martin Peters, 5 Alan Stephenson, 6 Bobby Moore (capt), 7 Harry Redknapp, 8 Ronnie Boyce, 9 Trevor Brooking, 10 Geoff Hurst, 11 John Sissons, 12 Jimmy Lindsay.

Scorers: Hurst 18, 34, 44, 48, 61, 71, Moore 26, Brooking 62
MoM: Geoff Hurst
West Ham ended the season: 8th out of 22, with 44 points.

Number: 31	1968-69	Division 1
2nd November 1968	Queens Park Rangers (h)	Att: 36,008

WEST HAM 4 QPR 3

This was the home fixture following Hurst's six-goal annihilation of Sunderland, which put another 12,000 on the gate. But instead of the predictable damp squib that many expected, a full house witnessed Upton Park's match of the season, a game televised by ITV London.

QPR were one of the most exciting sides seen in the First Division for years, playing a brand of open football that provided a hatful of goals – even though they would be relegated at the end of their first season in the top flight with just eighteen points. They never compromised on manager Alec Stock's open style of play, and would be back again in a few years, reaching second position in 1975-76, losing out on the title to Liverpool by a single point.

On this day, however, Hammers were in the ascendancy. Rangers were without their talisman Rodney Marsh, and West Ham were a step up in attitude after the 8-0 demolition of Sunderland. It was QPR who took the lead, though, with Bridges breaking free from Hazell's through pass and slipping it past Ferguson from his angled run. Nineteen minutes had passed. West Ham's equaliser was a stunner, Moore running out from defence, finding the Rangers midfield and defence parting like Bobby Charlton's hair, and hitting the ball from outside the area. Moore wandered back for the restart, apparently impervious to the emotion exhibited by his team-mates. Nine minutes later Redknapp's corner from the right was headed on by Brooking to Peters, who buried it in the corner with a header. The World Cup triumvirate completed their goal rush with West Ham's third three minutes later, Hurst heading home Moore's curling free-kick. None of the three Hammers' goalscorers managed a celebration more extravagent than a raised arm, though Brian Moore screamed out his TV commentary with gusto.

In the second half Rangers hit back, first Leach heading home Wilks' cross ten minutes after the turnaround, then ten minutes later heading Keen's left-wing cross over Ferguson for an equaliser. The winning goal was arguably the pick of the bunch, Redknapp hitting Hurst's left-wing cross on the volley from twenty yards.

Seven great goals, and with the other ten First Division matches only producing nine between them, this was the one to be at. Over the years, Hammers always seemed to enjoy entertaining matches against QPR, and this was certainly one of their best. As Michael Wale put it in *The Observer*: 'Here, in one match, is the reason why grown men become as children in the pursuit of a mere game.'

1 Bobby Ferguson, 2 Billy Bonds, 3 John Charles, 4 Martin Peters, 5 Alan Stephenson, 6 Bobby Moore (capt), 7 Harry Redknapp, 8 Ronnie Boyce, 9 Trevor Brooking, 10 Geoff Hurst, 11 Trevor Hartley,12 Jimmy Lindsay.

Scorers: Moore 30, Peters 39, Hurst 42, Redknapp 69
MoM: Harry Redknapp
West Ham ended the season: 8th out of 22, with 44 points.

| Number: 32 | 1968-69 | FA Cup R5 |
| 26th January 1969 | Mansfield Town (a) | Att: 21,117 |

MANSFIELD 3 WEST HAM 0

Yet another game from that 1968-69 season, but one that many fans would wish to forget – if they could. Defeat against a team from the Third Division, despite West Ham being at full strength and featuring the full World Cup Winning triumverate. Having said that, Mansfield had fought several successful encounters in the Cup to reach the fifth round, and to go one better was the footballing story of their season.

West Ham lay sixth in the First Division and hoped to reach the quarter finals of the Cup, as many top sides were already eliminated. They'd had a pretty easy ride thus far, knocking out Second Division basement club Bristol City at home 3-2, and then Huddersfield away, from the same division, 2-0. The last time they had made the last eight had been when winning the competition in 1964. With the World Cup Three in evidence. as well as the side unbeaten in 1969, over-confidence was in abundant supply. The tie itself had been postponed five times before going ahead on the evening of Wednesday, 26th February 1969 in front of 21,117 at Field Mill. The ground was packed as never before in anticipation of a giant-slaying.

West Ham began well in the mud against the Third Division strugglers, Geoff Hurst having two shots on goal in the opening five minutes. Ten minutes later, Redknapp might have scored when he got on the end of a Brooking cross, but when he failed to keep his feet in the mud his scuffed shot skidded wide. Mansfield became more confident with every missed West Ham chance, and in the 23rd minute Dudley Roberts smacked the ball home from a right-wing cross by Jimmy Goodfellow.

There was something in the way the Hammers trudged back to the centre spot that suggested this might not be Mansfield's only goal of the game. It wasn't. Fifteen minutes later they were two up. Ray Keeley waited for Sharkey's left-wing cross and struck a ferocious volley that flew past Ferguson. Mansfield's opener had arrived with only their second attack, but now they were totally in command.

West Ham emerged from their half-time roasting by Greenwood, but Mansfield came at them with even more determination and put the outcome beyond doubt in the 51st minute, when Scottish forward Nick Sharkey thumped home a third. The Hammers looked around as if for someone to blame, but only a pitch-sized mirror would have answered that question. Despite there being almost half the game left, they could not string together more than three passes and rarely threatened Dave Hollins in the Mansfield goal.

Defeat was a major wake up call for West Ham, who won four of their next five league matches to put some pride back into the club's season.

1 Bobby Ferguson, 2 Billy Bonds, 3 Bobby Howe, 4 Martin Peters, 5 Alan Stephenson, 6 Bobby Moore (capt), 7 Harry Redknapp, 8 Jimmy Lindsay, 9 Trevor Brooking, 10 Geoff Hurst, 11 John Sissons, 12 Ronnie Boyce.

MoM: Any of the eleven Mansfield Town players
West Ham ended the season: 8th out of 22, with 44 points.

Number: 33	1969-70	Division 1
11th August 1969	Chelsea (h)	Att: 39,003

WEST HAM 2 CHELSEA 0

Chelsea had conceded four goals at Anfield on the opening day of the season, but must have fancied their chances of recovering with a point or two from their visit to West Ham two days later, especially as they had not lost at Upton Park for nearly four years.

The Blues' inability to sign any new players over the summer was a disappointment for their fans, but they began this Monday evening flood-lit fixture in confident manner, Ian Hutchinson twice looking to repeat his scoring effort in front of the Liverpool kop. Hammers, however, finishing a creditable eighth the previous season, looked dangerous from the word go, and Hurst in particular looked like a man on a mission, beating Bonetti with a splendid chip from the edge of the area, only to see his effort land in the top of the net.

The sky darkened as the warm, overcast evening drew in, and there were scuffles in the crowd at both ends as the police struggled to contain disturbances typical in those days. Once Peter Osgood had missed a golden chance when one on one with Ferguson, the home crowd launched into 'Bubbles' and a carnival atmosphere developed.

Despite the goalless first half, West Ham looked likely to score at any moment, but it was only halfway through the second half that they finally did so. Martin Peters dispossessed Osgood as the Chelsea striker looked to find Charlie Cooke on a Chelsea breakaway, and the 'Ghost', as Peters was often called, weaseled past Hollins and McCreadie before trickling the ball beyond Bonetti's outstretched hand. The effort had just enough power to cross the line before Dempsey could reach it. Five minutes before time came the goal of the match, the lively Hurst exchanging passes with Peters before thumping the ball into the Chelsea net.

72,000 fans wached West Ham's first two games, both won without a goal conceded, and the side sat top of the league that evening. It was, of course, a temporary East London hiatus, and by the middle of September they found themselves on the edge of the relegation zone. Classic West Ham, in every sense of the words. Chelsea, however, had the last laugh this time, beating Leeds in the FA Cup final the following May.

1 Bobby Ferguson, 2 Billy Bonds, 3 John Charles, 4 Martin Peters, 5 Bobby Moore (capt), 6 Ronnie Boyce, 7 Harry Redknapp, 8 Jimmy Lindsay, 9 Peter Bennett, 10 Geoff Hurst, 11 John Sissons, 12 Bobby Howe.

Scorers: Geoff Hurst 65, Martin Peters 85
MoM: Martin Peters
West Ham ended the season: 17th out of 22, with 36 points.

Number: 34   1969-70   Division 1
21st March 1970   Manchester City (a)   Att: 28,353

MANCHESTER CITY 1 WEST HAM 5

The World Cup trio at Upton Park was now a duo; Martin Peters had left for Tottenham and would not be coming back. In his place, Jimmy Greaves, one of England's finest ever strikers, made his debut away at Manchester City on a pitch muddier than a Somme battlefield.

The sloppy sounds of players scampering around chasing the ball created an amusing audio backdrop, but not as amusing as the linesman's flag staying down when Pat Holland gathered the ball down the right, after City had committed themselves in attack, looking suspiciously offside. By the time the home defence had caught up, Hollnd had laid the ball across to Greaves who poked it in for one of the easiest goals he had ever scored.

Not that the statistical achievement wasn't notable – this was Greaves' fourth club debut and, as with Chelsea, AC Milan and Tottenham beforehand, he had now scored for West Ham in his first game. Justice was done, however, on the offside question when City soon equalised, Francis Lee's ambitious shot squirming under the feeble dive of Peter Grotier. Festoons of toilet rolls rained down from the crowd.

Greaves' second was even simpler, a ruck of players caught in the mud, and as the ball ran loose in the six-yard box Bobby Howe obligingly got out of the way so Greaves could tap in his second. West Ham's third was a peach. Boyce gathered the ball just inside the City half and aimed a perfect cross to the far post, where Hurst met it with a brave diving header. It was his 156th league goal for the Hammers, a post-war record in progress. So caked in mud was he, he could have been mistaken for a City player or even the referee.

Hurst and Greaves had in 1966 contested the role of England's No 1 striker, until the struggle had been settled by a World Cup final hat-trick.

They had even played together up front with three lions on their chest. Now they were reunited, and piling on the agony for Manchester City.

The goal of the game was scored by Ronnie Boyce. Joe Corrigan's drop kick reached Boyce advancing from the halfway line. He hit it back on the volley into the centre of the goal before Corrigan could get back. Never mind modern-day Beckham strikes from the halfway line, this was a Boyce special, hit with such ferocity that Corrigan could only stare at the bulge in the back of the net. Hammers wrapped the game up two minutes from time with another goal from Geoff Hurst. Bonds' cross dropped loose and Hurst hammered it in with his left foot.

1 Peter Grotier, 2 Billy Bonds, 3 Frank Lampard, 4 Ronnie Boyce, 5 Alan Stephenson, 6 Bobby Moore, 7 Pat Holland, 8 Peter Eustace, 9 Geoff Hurst, 10 Jimmy Greaves, 11 Bobby Howe, 12 David Llewellyn.

Scorers: Jimmy Greaves 10, 37, Geoff Hurst 45, 88, Ronnie Boyce 83
MoM: Ronnie Boyce
West Ham ended the season: 17th out of 22, with 36 points.

| Number: 35 | 1970-71 | Division 1 |
| 5th December 1970 | Derby County (a) | Att: 30,806 |

DERBY 2 WEST HAM 4

This was Jimmy Greaves' 500th Football League appearance, but it was Frank Wignall who opened the scoring for Derby in the eighth minute, firing in from just inside the area after dispossessing Eustace. The day was designed for the celebrating Greaves, however, and the legendary striker nipped past Mackay and Durban before slipping the ball past Les Green for the equaliser. West Ham, who had only won two of their opening nineteen league games, and both of those against the two clubs beneath them in the table, had been in disarray throughout the season. This would be the game that turned their fortunes around.

Trevor Brooking added a second three minutes later, on the counter from Derby, striding through and driving the ball into the corner. Derby manager Brian Clough was absent for reasons that were not publicised, but rudderless County pulled level when Durban fired home after another defensive error, this one from Tommy Taylor. With Hammers 19th and Derby 16th, this was a real chance for West Ham to claw themselves out of the relegation zone, but they missed several clear chances to restore their lead before half-time, Hurst and Greaves being the two principal offenders.

The second half saw a rejuvenated Derby, almost as if Clough had got on the phone to give them an earful. O'Hare and Hector had three gilt-edged chances early in the second half to put Derby ahead. The fifth goal of the game, when it came, was actually scored by Clyde Best, the Bermudan striker hammering home from twenty yards on a break out twenty minutes from time.

The tide of the game turned again, it appeared, when Derby were awarded a penalty ten minutes later for Eustace's challenge on Gemmill as he shaped to shoot. Bobby Ferguson, in his third game back since an eight-month lay off, guessed right and saved from Dave Mackay's kick. While Derby were bemoaning their lost equaliser, Best popped up in the right place at the right time to slot home West Ham's fourth.

Despite a welcome first away win, West Ham lost their next six games in a row, including a 0-4 drubbing at Blackpool, who had only won two Cup-ties in ten years. Derby, however, finished well, up in 9th spot. The following season they would win the league under Brian Clough. Jimmy Greaves also retired from football at the end of that season.

1 Bobby Ferguson, 2 Billy Bonds, 3 Frank Lampard, 4 Peter Eustace, 5 Tommy Taylor, 6 Bobby Moore (capt), 7 Jimmy Lindsay, 8 Trevor Brooking, 9 Clyde Best, 10 Geoff Hurst, 11 Jimmy Greaves, 12 Johnny Ayris.

Scorers: Jimmy Greaves 16, Trevor Brooking 19, Clyde Best 71, 88
MoM: Trevor Brooking
West Ham ended the season: 20th out of 22, with 34 points.

| Number: 36 | 1971-72 | League Cup QF |
| 17th November 1971 | Sheffield United (h) | Att: 36,834 |

WEST HAM 5 SHEFFIELD UNITED 0

The League Cup was a competition in which West Ham traditionally perform well, but despite an appearance in the final in 1966 against West Brom, when the final was played over home and away legs, they had never won it. Victories over Liverpool and Leeds in 1971-72 suggested this might be the year to change all that.

West Ham's performance against Sheffield United in the quarter-final remains one of their most emphatic Cup victories against top-division opposition. The fact that the Blades had won 2-1 at Upton Park eleven days earlier, with two goals from Gil Reece, and that they had not lost against London opposition for seven games, made this victory all the more satisfying.

The formation of the day was still 2-5-3, but Greenwood's approach had been moving towards the more continental 4-3-3. West Ham's three strikers, Best, Hurst and Robson, were a handful for any defence when they hit form. Unfortunately, with only two wins in seven in the league, this wasn't really happening. Bryan 'Pop' Robson had only scored twice in his previous thirteen games, so what happened next was an unexpected delight for all Hammers' fans.

Five minutes into the game Billy Bonds crossed from the right for Robson to score with a powerful header past John Hope. The second goal came on the half-hour from a pass by Hurst. Hovering outside the area, he threaded the ball through to Robson, whose turn and left-foot shot left Hope stranded. Hammers hit a third seven minutes later. Brooking found Best, who went wide on the right and hit a cross towards the far post looking for Bonds, only for the ball to drift over the keeper's head directly into the net. A third before half-time meant the Hammers were virtually certain to progress to the semi-finals.

The second half saw a continuation of the onslaught, but it took another half-hour before West Ham found the net again, despite shots raining in on Hope's goal. Clyde Best made it four from a free-kick by Bobby Moore that picked him out on the edge of the area. Best's ambitious volley went straight at Hope, but the keeper flapped at the ball before dropping it into the net. The power of the shot convinced everyone watching that it had to be given as Best's goal, and it was.

Three minutes before the end, Robson completed his hat-trick with the best goal of the game. Brooking curled a cross to the far post, where Robson knocked the ball down with his head and half-volleyed it with his right foot. A perfect hat-trick, in effect; a header, a left and then a right-foot finish to take the Hammers through to the semi-finals where they would meet Stoke for a place at Wembley in the New Year.

1 Bobby Ferguson, 2 John McDowell, 3 Frank Lampard, 4 Billy Bonds, 5 Tommy Taylor, 6 Bobby Moore (capt), 7 Harry Redknapp, 8 Clyde Best, 9 Geoff Hurst, 10 Trevor Brooking, 11 Bryan Robson, 12 Bobby Howe.

Scorers: Robson 5, 33, 87, Best 40, 76
MoM: Bryan Robson
West Ham ended the season: 14th of 22, with 36 points.

Number: 37   1971-72   League Cup SF2L
15th December 1971   Stoke City (h)   Att: 38,771

WEST HAM 0 STOKE 1

John Ritchie was Stoke's scorer when West Ham beat them in late September 1971. West Ham's goals were scored by Clyde Best and a shot by Bobby Moore that spooned over Gordon Banks off the heel of Stoke defender Denis Smith. Six weeks later they were paired against each other in the two-legged semi-final of the Football League Cup.

Hammers did the hard work in the first leg, winning 2-1 with a penalty blasted from Geoff Hurst and a neat finish from Clyde Best, following Harry Redknapp's perfectly weighted cross from the right. Stoke had scored first from Peter Dobing, but Hammers dominated thereafter and the scoreline at the end flattered Stoke more than it did West Ham. It didn't stop Dobing, the captain, declaring: 'Honestly, I still fancy us. We can play a whole lot better than we did, and I think West Ham are going to find out about it next week.'

The second leg, a week later, seemed a formality. Stoke had never won anything in their 108-year history and they would finish seventeenth in the league that season. No team losing the first leg of a League Cup semi-final had ever survived. Stoke had put out Southport, Oxford and Bristol Rovers, facing only one First Division side on their journey to the last four, that being Manchester United, and that needed two replays.

West Ham, unfortunately, played the game as though it was already won, and Dobing's words came back to haunt them. In truth they were rarely troubled by Stoke, but in a rare attack Tommy Taylor and John McDowell performed an 'after you, no after you', and Ritchie raced in to put Stoke ahead after 75 minutes, levelling the tie at 2-2.

Fate threw West Ham a lifeline when Banks felled Redknapp, who had slipped past Mike Pejic. This was Hammers' second penalty of the tie, this one right in front of the North Bank. And this one, as things stood, was a passport into the final. Hurst v Banks. The scorer of a World Cup final hat-trick against the keeper who had saved Pele's header in the 1970 World Cup. Who would come off best? The advantage was surely with the taker. Such a vast canvas on which to spray the shot, the goalkeeper barely a second to work out what to do. Stay still? Guess and commit? Try to follow the ball as it left the penalty spot?

Back on the halfway line, Billy Bonds was on his haunches, facing his own goalkeeper, unwilling to watch. Hurst began his run up from the edge of the 'D' and hit the ball as hard as he could, to Banks' right. Not unlike the Pele save, Banks threw himself at the ball and got to it. The ball flew up off his fists and spooned over the bar. Hurst stared at Banks on the floor before him, and then at the net, as if certain the ball should be in there somewhere. No way could this man have saved that penalty. That save alone was worthy of a place in the final at Wembley. However, the game was still tied at 2-2, there was no away-goals rule to determine the matter in West Ham's favour, and the half-hour of extra-time could not settle the issue. There would be a one-off replay at a neutral venue to be decided upon later.

1 Bobby Ferguson, 2 John McDowell, 3 Frank Lampard, 4 Billy Bonds, 5 Tommy Taylor, 6 Bobby Moore (capt), 7 Harry Redknapp, 8 Clyde Best, 9 Geoff Hurst, 10 Trevor Brooking, 11 Bryan Robson, 12 Bobby Howe.

Scorers: Hurst missed penalty (89)
MoM: Harry Redknapp
West Ham ended the season: 14th out of 22, with 36 points.

| Number: 38 | 1971-72 | League Cup SF2R |
| 26th January 1972 | Stoke (Hillsborough) | Att: 49,247 |

STOKE 3 WEST HAM 2

What remains bizarre about the path towards this breathtaking second League Cup semi-final replay at Old Trafford in January 1972 was the goalless first replay at the beginning of the month. Despite two efforts from Clyde Best that Gordon Banks saved, the second from almost point-blank range, the game had seen few clear-cut opportunities. The boorish Stoke support booed Bobby Moore throughout because of a mistimed early tackle against Jimmy Greenhoff. Hammers had cultivated a more impressive route to the final, defeating Liverpool, Leeds (at Elland Road after a replay), Sheffield United and Cardiff. It was also a great cup year for London, with the other semi-final featuring Chelsea and Spurs. Either opponent was a mouthwatering prospect for the Hammers if they could get past Stoke in this challenging second replay.

Early on, Stoke's Terry Conroy challenged Ferguson for the ball, but Ferguson got there first. Following up, however, with a challenge that would bring a straight red card these days, Conroy left Ferguson concussed. After five groggy minutes the Hammers keeper had to leave the field. Stepping into the breach, Bobby Moore put on the green jersey and took up his position in goal with Ferguson off the field, and seemingly unlikely to return.

Moore survived for twenty minutes until Redknapp's throw back to McDowell found the right-back in two minds whether or not to pass back to Moore. His half-hearted defensive prod was intercepted by John Richie who McDowell brought down in his effort to clear up his own mistake. Another penalty in this strange match, and one that Bobby Moore would be facing.

In a mud-pie goalmouth, Micky Bernard stepped up to take the penalty. Moore guessed right and blocked the ball, but it splashed out of the puddles back to Bernard, and the thankful Stoke defender rifled the ball into the net.

With 360 minutes of the semi-final played, West Ham were not about to roll over. Billy Bonds played a one-two with Bryan Robson before hitting a left-footed shot that clipped a Stoke defender's heel to send it away from Banks and into the net. Six minutes later, Bonds crossed from the right and Brooking half-volleyed in from outside the area. In under ten minutes West Ham had turned the game on its head, and were ahead for the first time since the first leg. Another goal was soon on its way, Conroy linking up with Eastham to find Dobing, who poked the ball through a crowd of players to put Stoke level again, two minutes before half-time.

A loud cheer greeted Bobby Ferguson as he trotted out to start the second half. Hammers had already beaten Stoke 2-1 in the first game, and a repeat at Hillsborough would guarantee a first Wembley appearance for seven years. Stoke, however, came at West Ham. Bonds headed out Marsh's cross, but only to Conroy, who volleyed the ball into the net from fifteen yards. Stoke might have extended their lead, though it was West Ham, minutes before the end, who felt they should have been awarded a penalty when Pejic appeared to foul Hurst. Referee Partridge waved play on. West Ham lost 2-3.

Four games, two sessions of extra-time, and 420 minutes of football, surely this had been one of the greatest English cup-ties ever played. Both sides knew by the time of the second replay that the team awaiting them at Wembley was Chelsea, a prospect that all Hammers fans relished. As it was, one pleasing outcome was that Stoke would lift their first ever trophy by beating Chelsea 2-1, so West Ham could at least say they were beaten by the eventual winners of the tournament.

1 Bobby Ferguson, 2 John McDowell, 3 Frank Lampard, 4 Billy Bonds, 5 Tommy Taylor, 6 Bobby Moore (capt), 7 Harry Redknapp, 8 Clyde Best, 9 Geoff Hurst, 10 Trevor Brooking, 11 Brian Robson, 12 Peter Eustace.

Scorers: Billy Bonds 39, Trevor Brooking 46
MoM: Billy Bonds
West Ham ended the season: 14th out of 22, with 36 points.

Number: 39	1972-73	Division 1
19th August 1972	Leicester City (h)	Att: 25,414

WEST HAM 5 LEICESTER 2

This seven goals and no bookings spectacle was described by many who saw it as one of the best games of attacking football seen at Upton Park for many years. Leicester came out from the kick-off with goals on their mind, and Mike Stringfellow fired them ahead after just two minutes with a shot from just inside the West Ham area.

Bobby Moore, whose goals over a fifteen-year West Ham career were few and far between, made an excursion upfield ten minutes later to finish off a move involving Bonds and Brooking and level the score. West Ham knocked the ball around entertainingly, Coker and Robson coming close, but it was Leicester who scored next, Len Glover wrong-footing Ferguson after good approach work from Sammels.

That was pretty much it for Leicester. The Hammers grew in confidence, sensing the game was there for the taking. With Best, Robson and the young Ade Coker looking to iron over concerns about lack of firepower after the departure of Geoff Hurst (Best had outscored Hurst by seven the previous season), Hammers had a point to prove, and they certainly proved it. Coker squared things up again with a confident finish six minutes after Glover had put Leicester in front.

With the scores level at the break, cynics might have anticipated a second half that wouldn't match the entertainment value. Instead, what followed showcased West Ham at their very best. Moore was the showmaker, the distribution king, as first Tyler and then Brooking teed up opportunities for the Hammers' front three. When West Ham took the lead for the first time in the match it was through Bryan Robson predatory finish, following a run to the byline by Tyler. Robson returned the favour, when he might have had a shot himself, setting up Tyler for the fourth.

A fifth goal arrived ten minutes from time, when Robson hit his second past Peter Shilton. Rarely can a goalkeeper conceding five goals in a game have played so flawlessly, but on the day West Ham could probably have overcome any team unfortunate enough to have had to face them at Upton Park in this form.

1 Bobby Ferguson, 2 John McDowell, 3 Frank Lampard, 4 Billy Bonds, 5 Tommy Taylor, 6 Bobby Moore (capt), 7 Dudley Tyler, 8 Clyde Best, 9 Ade Coker, 10 Trevor Brooking, 11 Bryan Robson, 12 Ronnie Boyce.

Scorers: Moore 17, Coker 38, Robson 53, 78, Tyler 70
MoM: Bobby Moore
West Ham ended the season: 6th out of 22, with 46 points.

Number: 40	1972-73	Division 1
14th April 1973	Leeds United (h)	Att: 38,804

WEST HAM 1 LEEDS 1

The Hammers had faced champions-to-be Leeds in 1971 while flirting with relegation. Two years later they went into the Leeds fixture on the back of four straight wins that had launched them into fifth position, with Leeds just above them in third. This game, however, was to be remembered for other reasons.

Leeds' pedigree front line of Allan Clarke, Peter Lorimer and Mick Jones were kept at bay by the defence of Moore, Bonds, Lampard and McDowell, with Hammers' efforts at goal coming from 'Pop' Robson, scorer of 25 goals, and Ted MacDougall with four in five games since joining the Hammers. Though goalless at half-time, it seemed impossible that the game should finish that way.

Fifteen minutes into the second half came the incident that would disfigure the game. After a deep cross to the far post from Johnny Giles, Ferguson leapt to gather the ball beyond Jones and Bates but went over backwards after clipping John McDowell's shoulder. The goalkeeper landed upside down, spilling the ball and looking as though he might have broken his neck. The ground fell silent and a macabre hush descended. The St John Ambulance Men and the physio clearly feared the worst. The size of the medical cluster around Ferguson had the crowd guessing from the gestures of the ambulance men and gesticulations of the players. Of all the games to televise, the BBC had picked this one, pictures that would be shown later that evening on *Match of the Day*.

Ferguson got the biggest cheer of the day some ten minutes later once he'd got to his feet. He was helped off the pitch and Bertie Lutton came on to replace him. A year earlier Ferguson's concussion against Stoke had led to Moore taking over in goal. Now it was Clyde Best who volunteered. The big Bermudan did well initially, making a couple of regulation saves and clearing well. However, the Leeds pressure eventually began to tell and West Ham, still clearly shaken by events, fell behind seven minutes from the end when Clarke ran in to head Leeds in front.

Deep into stoppage time, all fifteen minues of it, Pat Holland forced home a deserved equaliser. The crowd celebrated the moment, but were still talking about Ferguson's injury long after the final whistle.

Though he missed the following two games, Ferguson's injury was not life-threatening, and he resurfaced for the last two fixtures, against Birmingham away and Arsenal at home. His temporary replacement, Peter Grotier, whose previous eight-month stint during the 1970-71 season had been to cover Ferguson's long injury lay-off, never played for the Hammers' first team again.

Bryan Robson finished top scorer with 28 goals, but despite his good start, Ted MacDougall, signed from Manchester United for £150,000, played just 25 games for the club, scoring only six goals. In those days, £6,000 a game looked like a bad deal.

1 Bobby Ferguson, 2 John McDowell, 3 Frank Lampard, 4 Billy Bonds, 5 Kevin Lock, 6 Bobby Moore (capt), 7 Clyde Best, 8 Pat Holland, 9 Ted MacDougall, 10 Trevor Brooking, 11 Bryan Robson, 12 Bertie Lutton.

Scorers: Pat Holland 90
MoM: Bobby Moore
West Ham ended the season: 6th out of 22, with 46 points.

GAME 6 Bolton 2 West Ham 0, April 1923
(Jimmy Ruffell struggles with the Empire Stadium divots)

GAME 13 West Ham 1 Blackburn 0, June 1940
(Barron's mistake lets in Sammy Small)

GAME 25 Liverpool 1 West Ham 2, September 1963
(Furnell grabs the ball in front of Peter Brabrook)

GAME 27 West Ham 2 TSV Munich 1860 0, May 1965
(Sealey's stunner gives the Hammers the lead at Wembley)

GAME 36 West Ham 5 Sheffield United 0, November 1971
(Bonds shepherds Best's cross over the line)

GAME 37 West Ham 0 Stoke 1, December 1971
(Banks beats away Hurst's penalty)

GAME 38 Stoke 3 West Ham 2, January 1972
(Moore misses the rebound after saving Bernard's spot-kick)

GAME 39 West Ham 5 Leicester 2, August 1972
(Bryan Robson finally puts the Hammers in front against Leicester)

GAME 40
West Ham 1 Leeds 1,
April 1973 (Clyde Best in
goal against Leeds after
Bobby Ferguson's injury)

GAME 43 West Ham 5 Wolverhampton 2, November 1974
(a spectacular finish against Wolves from Trevor Brooking)

GAME 44 Arsenal 0 West Ham 2, March 1975
(Taylor makes it safe for West Ham at Highbury)

GAME 45
West Ham 2 Fulham 0,
May 1975 (Six-shooter Alan
Taylor celebrates West Ham's
1975 FA Cup win)

GAME 46 Den Haag 4 West Ham 2, March 1976
(Jennings' brace sets up the second leg against Den Haag)

GAME 47 West Ham 3 Eintracht Frankfurt 1, April 1976
(Brooking heads for the sky to put Hammers ahead v Eintracht Frankfurt)

GAME 48 Arsenal 2 West Ham 3, February 1977
(Taylor nips in to grab the equaliser at Highbury)

GAME 51 West Ham 0 Nottingham Forest 0, December 1979
(Bonds and Cross watch Devonshire's effort narrowly miss the target)

GAME 52 Arsenal 0 West Ham 1, May 1980
(The underdogs celebrate their finest ever victory over Arsenal)

GAME 53 Liverpool 1 West Ham 1, March 1981
(Ray Stewart grabs Hammers a deserved replay from the penalty-spot)

GAME 55 West Ham 5 Birmingham 0, September 1982
(Alvin Martin hits an untypical but effective volley to make it 4-0)

GAME 61 West Ham 2 Liverpool 2, August 1985
(Devonshire puts McAvennie through to score West Ham's first)

GAME 62 Chelsea 0 West Ham 4, March 1986
(Devonshire in command as the Hammers ride roughshod over Chelsea)

GAME 63 West Ham 8 Newcastle 1, April 1986
(Alvin Martin completes his hat-trick from the penalty spot)

GAME 72 West Ham 1 Manchester United 0, April 1992
(Mitchell Thomas salutes Kenny Brown's unexpected winner)

GAME 74 West Ham 5 Oxford United 3, November 1992
(Julian Dicks smashes home his second goal)

GAME 76   Blackburn 0 West Ham 2, September 1993
(Trevor Morley scores while lying on the pitch)

GAME 77   Tottenham 1 West Ham 4, April 1994
(A brilliant individual finish from Trevor Morley at White Hart Lane)

GAME 78 West Ham 3 Manchester City 0, December 1994
(Tony Cottee strokes home the first of three against Manchester City)

GAME 80 West Ham 3 Coventry 2, January 1996
(Frank Lampard introduced on debut by Uncle Harry)

GAME 81 West Ham 4 Manchester City 2, March 1996
(Iain Dowie upsets former manager Alan Ball with a powerful header)

GAME 82 West Ham 4 Tottenham 3, February 1997
(Julian Dicks plays god in the rain from Michael Hughes' corner)

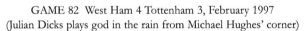

GAME 84 West Ham 6 Barnsley 0, January 1998
(Samassi Abou flicks home Moncur's pass to make it 3-0)

GAME 85 West Ham 3 Wimbledon 4, September 1998
(Ian Wright makes it two inside a quarter of an hour against Wimbledon)

GAME 86 FC Metz 1 West Ham 3, August 1999
(Lampard atones for the penalty miss from the first leg)

GAME 88 West Ham 5 Bradford City 4, February 2000
(Joe Cole hits his debut goal at Upton Park to make it 4-4)

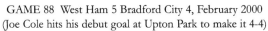

GAME 89   West Ham 5 Charlton 0, December 2000
(Trevor Sinclair hits a Boxing Day goal of festive genius against Charlton)

GAME 90
Man Utd 0 West Ham 1,
January 2001
(Paolo Di Canio just can't
help it – he's brilliant!)

GAME 91 Charlton 4 West Ham 4, November 2001
(Paul Kitson shows there's life in the old boy yet)

GAME 92 Chelsea 2 West Ham 3, September 2002
(You won't see too many people score a goal like that at Stamford Bridge)

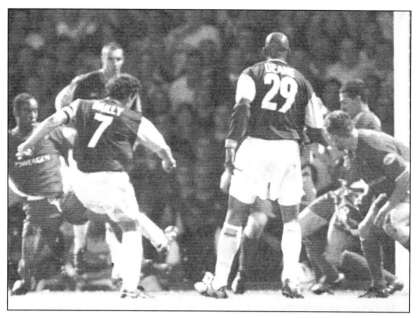

GAME 94 West Ham 2 Ipswich 0, May 2004
(Christian Dailly hits a vital pea-roller against Ipswich to make it 2-0)

GAME 95 Ipswich 0 West Ham 2, May 2005
(Bobby Zamora has his sights firmly set on Cardiff now!)

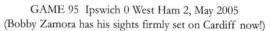

GAME 97 Liverpool 3 West Ham 3, May 2006
(FA Cup final genius from Dean Ashton)

GAME 98 Manchester United 0 West Ham 1, May 2007
(Carlos Tevez makes Premier League safety a reality)

GAME 99 West Ham 2 Manchester United 1, December 2007
(Matthew Upson celebrates his winner against Manchester United)

GAME 101 West Ham 4 Blackburn 1, August 2008
(Craig Bellamy volleys home to bury Blackburn in injury-time)

Number: 41   1973-74   Division 1
26th December 1973   Chelsea (a)   Att: 26,982

CHELSEA 2 WEST HAM 4

Christmas might be a time for resting at home with the family and for a
turkey binge that lasts several days. The last thing any family expect is for
dad to forsake them on Boxing Day in favour of a football match kicking off at 11am, for which he has had to rise at an unseasonal hour and
from which he may return incalculably late. Boxing Day 1973 was such a
day for many West Ham fans, and a day they would never forget.

Just before Christmas, minus the unfit Moore, Brooking, Bryan
Robson and the suspended Billy Bonds, Hammers had taken on Stoke.
Mick McGiven arrived on loan from Sunderland, and Graham Paddon
played his third game for the club. The Hammers lost 0-2, the atmos-
phere possessing nothing particularly festive, making it just one West
Ham win in nine games.

The other side of Christmas, however, promised better, with the missing players (with the exception of Bonds) all returning. With West Ham
21st in the league, they needed something special to be pulled out of the
bag, or cracker.

Chelsea could have been excused for thinking Christmas had arrived
a day late. By half-time they had run up a 2-0 lead, with goals from Ian
Britton and Alan Hudson, a score which did nothing to flatter their
supremacy. Frank Lampard, however, produced one of his magical turns
just after half-time with an angled shot, catching Bonetti off his line and
bringing Hammers unexpectedly back into contention. It should have
been 3-1 a few minutes later, when Peter Osgood somehow hit the bar
from eight yards out. From the rebound, Hammers broke away and a
four-man move culminated with Bobby Gould slotting home an unlikely
equaliser. Six minutes on, Clyde Best converted Brooking's pass to complete the comeback. With almost half an hour remaining, it seemed just
a matter of time before Chelsea settled and got their game back together again, but try as they might, they could not direct more than a couple
of shots on Day's goal. To add insult to injury, Best, who seemed to make
a habit of scoring goals in twos, hit a second six minutes from time on
the counter, giving Hammers a 4-2 victory.

West Ham would lose at Tottenham three days later, with two late
goals from Pratt and Chivers, but the New Year saw excellent league form
that finally carried them clear of the guaranteed relegation position they
had occupied just before Christmas.

1 Mervyn Day, 2 Keith Coleman, 3 Frank Lampard, 4 John McDowell, 5 Tommy Taylor, 6 Bobby Moore (capt), 7 Mick McGiven, 8 Graham Paddon, 9 Bobby Gould, 10 Trevor Brooking, 11 Clyde Best.

Scorers: Lampard 48, Gould 57, Best 63, 84
MoM: Clyde Best
West Ham ended the season: 18th out of 22, with 37 points.

Number: 42   1973-74   Division 1
27th April 1974   Liverpool (h)   Att: 36,160

WEST HAM 2 LIVERPOOL 2

A disappointing season for West Ham, after the dizzy heights of sixth in 72-73, ended with a not untypical do-or-die contest against Liverpool. Bill Shankly's men had already conceded the championship to Leeds but were keen to finish the season with a win. West Ham knew they had to perform well and hope that Southampton, Birmingham and Chelsea slipped up, now that the bottom three clubs went down for the first time. Manchester United and Norwich were already doomed. It just remained to be seen who would join them in the Second Division.

The unusual aspect to Hammers' run-in was that for the first time since 1957-58 it was undertaken without Bobby Moore, who'd played his last game for the Hammers in the FA Cup against Hereford in the calamitous 1-1 draw back in January. Hammers had been bottom after eleven games but recovered without the injured Moore with ten unbeaten games between January and March. These included a home win over eventual champions Leeds. Moore left for Fulham in mid-March 1974.

Now, on the last day of the season, they were again up against it, facing the side that had booted them from the League Cup back in October. Keith Coleman returned at right-back and John McDowell had moved into midfield, which seemed to work for Greenwood, though Hammers had only managed two draws from their previous three games.

Liverpool started brightly but were stunned in the 32nd minute when Frank Lampard hit a shot from 25 yards that should have had Fyffes written on it. The ball began its journey off-target, but bent inwards to plant itself in the top corner of Ray Clemence's goal. In the classic sedentary pose adopted by goalkeepers when beaten by the unsavables, Clemence was a picture of disbelief. Facing a Liverpool penalty seven minutes later was Mervyn Day, a teenage replacement for Bobby Ferguson, who had moaned about too many 'spineless' and 'gutless' men in the team. Day saved Alec Lindsay's spot-kick to keep the Hammers in front at half-time. There was nothing 'spineless' or 'gutless' about Day on this particular afternoon.

This was the Liverpool captained by Emlyn Hughes, with Toshack and Keegan good for goals anywhere. Toshack proved he didn't just score with his head with a delightful chip to beat Day on the hour. Then, if Lampard's goal was a bolt from the blue, Trevor Brooking emulated the feat with a volley from the edge of the area. Clemence's expression this time made one wonder whether he might have missed out on a career in stand-up comedy.

The transistor radios were on all around the ground, as fans listened to the results. It was soon clear that if Hammers could hang on, they would be safe. Any West Ham fan will admit to the frequency of such moments over the years, and Liverpool's refusal to lie down told in the last minute, when a cross to the far post saw Keegan, proving he didn't score just with his feet, head past Day to equalise.

Upton Park fell silent, and the expression on the defenders' faces said it all. They needn't have worried. Birmingham's inferior goal figures and the point the Hammers had gained meant that even though Southampton had won 3-0 at Everton, West Ham escaped the drop.

Another curiosity of the season was Billy Bonds' move into midfield. This helped him become both Hammer of the Year and the club's top scorer with thirteen goals, sharing the honour with Clyde Best.

1 Mervyn Day, 2 Keith Coleman, 3 Frank Lampard, 4 Billy Bonds (capt), 5 Tommy Taylor, 6 John McDowell, 7 Pat Holland, 8 Graham Paddon, 9 Bobby Gould, 10 Trevor Brooking, 11 Clyde Best.

Scorers: Frank Lampard 32, Trevor Brooking 67
MoM: Mervyn Day
West Ham ended the season: 18th out of 22, with 37 points.

Number: 43   1974-75   Division 1
16th November 1974 Wolverhampton (h)   Att: 31,708

WEST HAM 5 WOLVERHAMPTON 2

This was the first of three seasons where John Lyall took the reins with Ron Greenwood, laying the foundations for his own particular style of football. By the time of Wolves' visit, Hammers had only lost once in ten games, and Billy Jennings and Keith Robson had arrived from Watford and Newcastle respectively. Just four points off the leaders, Hammers turned on a majestic performance.

The piratically bearded Bonds opened the scoring eight minutes before half-time with a penalty, after Brooking's cross had been handled, rifling the spot-kick low into the left-hand corner past Phil Parkes. A minute before half-time Keith Robson's cross was flicked on by Gould to Brooking, who finished coolly under the keeper.

Two up at the break, Hammers continued the onslaught with a neat free-kick. Brooking teed up Lampard to volley through the Wolves' wall. Steve Kindon then beat the Hammers' offside trap, putting Richards in for a Wolves' reply, before Jennings hit a fourth, turning in the loose ball after Parkes had failed to keep out Brooking's volley. Jennings boasted a distinctive goal celebration, years before they became a peculiar art form. He would fall to his knees and issue some kind of thankful prayer, followed by an excited, smiling, nodding expression, waving both fists together. It didn't catch on, but as the leading scorer that season with fourteen, he had plenty of opportunities to try it out and refine it.

Hammers' final goal was scored by Bobby Gould against his old club, after Brooking had put him through. Wolves were left with five minutes to score a second consolation, accredited to Steve Kindon's neat header.

1 Mervyn Day, 2 Keith Coleman, 3 Frank Lampard, 4 Billy Bonds, 5 Tommy Taylor, 6 Kevin Lock, 7 Billy Jennings, 8 Graham Paddon, 9 Bobby Gould, 10 Trevor Brooking, 11 Keith Robson.

Scorers: Bonds 37p, Brooking 44, Lampard 62, Jennings 78, Gould 85
MoM: Trevor Brooking
West Ham ended the season: 13th out of 22, with 39 points.

Number: 44	1974-75	FA Cup QF
8th March 1975	Arsenal (a)	Att: 56,742

ARSENAL 0 WEST HAM 2

Cup-ties often produce contests that league fixtures cannot compete with, so strong is the reward. A cup final day at Wembley with 100,000 watching is something few footballers experience. And the nearer it gets, the more the tension mounts.

To reach their 1975 moment, West Ham had to fight some tough games, including this brawl at Highbury in the mud. It might not have been a contest for purists, but was nevertheless a cracking London derby that few fans of either side would forget.

Both sides started well, despite the swamp-like conditions, but a quarter of an hour in, Keith Robson pushed the ball to Billy Jennings. The ball stuck in the mud, Jennings missed it, the clearance ran to Paddon, who pulled it back across goal where Alan Taylor hammered it into the roof of the net. The haphazardness of the goal was further dramatised by Taylor's leap into the net, where he hung pendulously on the netting before his team-mates descended upon him in celebration. For Arsenal fans, the goal having being scored in front of the North Bank, it must have seemed their stars had drifted into the wrong hemisphere. Arsenal's fading lights had met with Alan Taylor rising. This was hardly contradicted by the superb save Day made from Matthews' skidding shot ten minutes later. Then, with John Radford through on 45 minutes, Day seemed to bring him down, but referee Burns waved away Arsenal's protests.

A minute after the change-round, Arsenal began another move that ended with Matthews hitting a left-footer towards the far corner. Day scrambled across his goal to claw the ball away. From the resulting breakaway Taylor hit his second, after exchanging passes with Brooking on the slippery surface. Taylor's strike flew past Jimmy Rimmer into the bottom corner. There was little sight of grass on the mudslop pitch that afternoon, and even less sight of red and white scarves in the fading minutes.

1 Mervyn Day, 2 John McDowell, 3 Frank Lampard, 4 Billy Bonds (capt), 5 Tommy Taylor, 6 Kevin Lock, 7 Billy Jennings, 8 Graham Paddon, 9 Alan Taylor, 10 Trevor Brooking, 11 Keith Robson, 12 Bobby Gould.

Scorers: Alan Taylor 15, 46
MoM: Trevor Brooking
West Ham ended the season: 13th out of 22, with 39 points.

| Number: 45 | 1974-75 | FA Cup final |
| 8th May 1975 | Fulham (Wembley) | Att: 100,000 |

WEST HAM 2 FULHAM 0

West Ham had met Second Division Fulham, captained by Bobby Moore, in the cup on 8th October 1974. That was the League Cup, however, and

West Ham were knocked out 1-2. Leading 1-0 at half-time from a Trevor Brooking goal, the floodlights had failed and, when they were restored, one of the four corners stayed dark. That was at Mervyn Day's end in the second half. Referee Howard New offered to play on or call the match off. Day said continue, and was promptly beaten by two soft goals that effectively eliminated the Hammers.

To play Fulham again, seven months later, was a curious coincidence that wouldn't have been lost on Bobby Moore, in his first full season away from his only other club. A football legend in his own lifetime, now alongside another ex-England international in his twilight years, Alan Mullery, Moore might have thought he was about to be part of an incredible football happening. Second Division Sunderland had overcome mighty Leeds at Wembley two years earlier. These were times of giant killings, and West Ham looked beatable, having won just once in nine attempts in the league, and only three times in the previous five months.

Chelsea and Spurs had played out a tame London derby FA Cup final in 1967, so it was hardly guaranteed that two London sides would fare any better in the entertainment stakes. The difference was that players old and young had points to prove in this final. Alan Taylor had begun the season playing for Fourth Division Rochdale. £40,000 and six months later, he was in the West Ham first team at Wembley, having scored the four goals that had taken them through the quarter-final and semi-finals against Arsenal and Ipswich.

The first half was played at a furious pace and seemed to have 'shock' written all over it. Shots and headers rained in from Fulham's Cutbush, Lacy, Busby and Conway, but West Ham held their nerve and got to half-time on level terms. Three second-half minutes settled the game, the first when Billy Jennings, set up by Pat Holland, fired in a shot from twenty yards that Peter Mellor spilled. Alan Taylor goal-poached in the six-yard box to put West Ham ahead. Three minutes later Paddon, put through wide on the left by Holland, hit an oblique shot that Mellor obligingly dropped into the path of Alan Taylor, who completed his third brace in three Cup-ties to become West Ham's tournament 'six shooter' and match winner.

Despite Fulham having almost half an hour to recover, Bonds, Lock and Tommy Taylor tightened things up and made it almost impossible for Fulham to advance within shooting distance of Mervyn Day's goal. So in the end it wasn't to be for West Ham's greatest ever captain Bobby Moore or his Fulham team. It was the players he had nurtured at West Ham who mounted the Wembley steps to gather the FA Cup, eleven years after Moore himself had raised it after West Ham's 1964 victory over Preston.

1 Mervyn Day, 2 John McDowell, 3 Frank Lampard, 4 Billy Bonds (capt),
5 Tommy Taylor, 6 Kevin Lock, 7 Billy Jennings, 8 Graham Paddon, 9
Alan Taylor, 10 Trevor Brooking, 11 Pat Holland, 12 Bobby Gould.

Scorers: Alan Taylor 61, 64
MoM: Billy Bonds
West Ham ended the season: 13th out of 22, with 39 points.

Number: 46	1975-76	CWC QF 1L
3rd March 1976	Den Haag (a)	Att: 26,000

DEN HAAG 4 WEST HAM 2

With Brooking out and Lyall down with flu, Ron Greenwood had to take
the reins for this tough quarter-final first leg in Holland. The German referee, Rudi Glockner, had officiated at the 1970 World Cup final between
Brazil and Italy, but his decisions on this evening looked at one stage as
if they would cost West Ham the tie.

One thing not in dispute was Den Haag's opener, scored by their
defender and captain Aad Mansveld, thirteen minutes into the game. The
Hammers' defending was atrocious as Den Haag piled bodies into an all-
out attack which culminated with a captain's shot from the edge of the
area that Day appeared not to see. Two minutes later McDowell controlled a long ball into the Hammers' area with his chest before clearing,
only to see Glockner award a penalty against him. The captain Mansveld
took it, driving it home to Day's right.

Hammers had clearly been wrong-footed by the refereeing error and
could offer little up front for Billy Jennings, a lone striker for most of the
first half. When Simon van Vliet ran at goal, Lock's tackle cut out a lump
of turf in the box although the Den Haag defender appeared to trip over
his own feet. The referee was barely up with the play, but still saw enough
to give a second penalty. Mansveld completed his hat-trick with this one,
sending Day the wrong way.

Despite what had gone before, the worst refereeing decision was still
to come. Three minutes before the break, Paddon prepared to take a free-
kick in midfield, not realising the referee had stopped play for a drop ball
after an earlier collision. Instead of telling the player his decision, the referee bounced the ball in front of Paddon, who stood motionless and perplexed. Seizing the moment, Lex Schoenmaker dashed between Glockner
and Paddon, the ball at his feet. Even the cameras stayed with Paddon

and the referee, presuming the ball would be returned. It never was. Den Haag played on, and after an unintentional one-two with an equally confused Billy Bonds, Schoenmaker tapped the ball into the net. Despite furious protests from West Ham, the goal stood.

This was West Ham's first venture into Europe for eleven years, and it was about to end in farce. John Lyall, from his sick bed, had put out the best team he and Ron Greenwood could raise, yet a catalogue of refereeing decisions had left them 0-4 down at the interval. To go through, they would need to score five at Upton Park, and even then only if they were able to stop the Dutch team scoring more goals in the second half. What chance of that?

The match was broadcast on BBC Radio that evening, but because of programme scheduling only the second half was covered live. Therefore the first thing every West Ham fan tuning in discovered was that their side was 0-4 down and it was only half-time! There must have been many who simply turned their radios off, not bothering to listen to what was clearly going to develop into a rout.

Those who stayed heard different. Whether through over-confidence or embarrassment at the riches of refereeing errors, Den Haag were vulnerable. Whatever the cause, it was soon a completely different game.

Hammers' makeshift defence looked more organised after McGiven was replaced by Coleman. West Ham began to string passes together and Den Haag began to look complacent at the back. After 50 minutes Paddon pulled the ball low into the six-yard box, where Billy Jennings, the only West Ham shirt among five Den Haag defenders, sent the ball past Ton Thie in the Dutch goal, despite the keeper getting a full hand on it. Eight minutes later came the goal of the game. Paddon again, marauding down the left, again with just Jennings to aim at. A perfect cross floated over the Den Haag defenders into Jennings' near-post position, and the tiny striker headed into the top right-hand corner.

There was still half an hour remaining, and it was now all West Ham, the Den Haag keeper turning away fierce shots from Robson and Alan Taylor. Jennings might have completed a memorable hat-trick five minutes from time had he achieved any meaningful contact with Alan Curbishley's curling cross.

With two away goals, a West Ham win by 2-0 or 3-1 would be enough to take them to their third Cup-Winners' Cup semi-final. And when Den Haag came to Upton Park for the second leg, that was exactly what happened. In a curious echo of the first game, West Ham scored all three of their goals in the first half, Den Haag replying with their single strike on the hour, and then no further goals in the last 30 minutes.

1 Mervyn Day, 2 Mick McGiven, 3 Frank Lampard, 4 Billy Bonds (capt), 5 Tommy Taylor, 6 Kevin Lock, 7 Alan Taylor, 8 Graham Paddon, 9 Billy Jennings, 10 Alan Curbishley, 11 Keith Robson, 12 Keith Coleman.

Scorers: Billy Jennings 50, 58
MoM: Graham Paddon
West Ham ended the season: 18th out of 22, with 36 points.

| Number: 47 | 1975-76 | CWC SF1L2 |
| 14th April 1976 | Eintracht Frankfurt (h) | Att: 39,202 |

WEST HAM 3 EINTRACHT FRANKFURT 1

There have been few games at Upton Park as exciting or prestigious as the second leg of this European Cup-Winners' Cup-tie against Eintracht in April 1976. West Ham had lost the first leg 1-2 a fortnight previously, so there was still everything to play for.

West Ham fielded the same eleven. They might have been strong in Europe but they were weak in the league, sixteen games without a win. In fact their last First Division win was 1-0 over QPR on 24th January 1976. But then they could still turn it on under the floodlights in Europe.

These were the days of 90 yards of thinning green and two giant cow-pat goalmouths. West Ham started off strongly on a miserably wet night and Keith Robson had the ball in the net early on, only to see his effort ruled out for an over-zealous challenge on the keeper.

West Ham took the lead five minutes into the second half when Frank Lampard's hanging cross was headed in by Trevor Brooking, whose timed jump reversed the trajectory of the ball to send it into the far corner of the net. The Frankfurt side came back with urgency, and Wanzel's shot was turned round the post by Day. Five minutes later another effort was cleared off the line by Coleman after Korbel had hit the post.

West Ham then released themselves from the siege to score a second, putting them ahead on aggregate, and what a goal it was. Breaking from defence, Brooking hit a 30-yard pass to Keith Robson, whose first touch was poor and produced groans from the crowd. But Robson flicked the ball forward and hit an unstoppable 30-yard effort into the top corner. It was almost as if he had deliberately miscontrolled the ball to lull the keeper into a false sense of security.

Five minutes later Frankfurt almost squared the tie when Grabowski hit a piledriver which Day turned away for a corner. Now it was Paddon's turn to play the creator, his through ball finding Brooking, who stepped past two defenders before giving Hammers a 3-0 lead on the night. It seemed an improbable score, given how combative the opposition had been.

Those three goals proved vital as Beverungen scored for the Germans with three minutes remaining. Another goal would have squeezed them through on away goals, but Hammers held fast to reach their second Cup-Winners' final. Brussels' Heysel stadium had been selected as the venue back in the summer, which proved unfortunate for West Ham when local side Anderlecht also reached the final. West Ham had enjoyed 'home' advantage back in 1965 over TSV Munich 1860, so this evened things out. In the event, West Ham lost 2-4.

1 Mervyn Day, 2 Keith Coleman, 3 Frank Lampard, 4 Billy Bonds (capt), 5 Tommy Taylor, 6 John McDowell, 7 Pat Holland, 8 Graham Paddon, 9 Billy Jennings, 10 Trevor Brooking, 11 Keith Robson.

Scorers: Trevor Brooking 49, 78, Keith Robson 67
MoM: Mervyn Day / Trevor Brooking
West Ham ended the season: 18th out of 22, with 36 points.

Number: 48	1976-77	Division 1
19th February 1977	Arsenal (a)	Att: 38,221

ARSENAL 2 WEST HAM 3

This was an era that saw West Ham enjoy several precious wins over the 'Gooners', including an FA Cup quarter-final victory at muddy Highbury on their way to Cup triumph at Wembley, and a Cup final win as Second Division underdogs in 1980. Another Highbury victory against the odds came in 1976-77, the manner of which was as delightful as the win itself.

West Ham differed from their 1975 side considerably, featuring four new signings: Anton Otulakowski, John Radford, Bill Green and the sublime Alan Devonshire, rescued from non-league Southall for a magnificent career that was to unfold in the decade ahead.

Liam Brady, also with his career unfolding, put Arsenal ahead in the thirteenth minute. Although West Ham had gained a reputation for failing to score once they fell behind, this time they hit back ten minutes later. Brooking stroked a pass to Alan Taylor, who had timed his run to stay onside, and he sidestepped Cooper to give himself the simplest of tap-ins and his fifth goal of the season. Ten minutes later, Brooking hit a free-kick to the far post, where John Radford's goalbound header was flicked in by Billy Jennings.

Trailing at half-time, Arsenal levelled when Frank Stapleton finished off a four-man move. On the counter from an Arsenal side hunting a winner, Lampard delivered a cross to the near post which Alan Taylor met with a diving header. A quarter of an hour remained, but Hammers defended resolutely to avenge the 1-6 thrashing suffered at Highbury a year earlier.

1 Mervyn Day, 2 Billy Bonds (capt), 3 Frank Lampard, 4 Anton Otulakowski, 5 Bill Green, 6 Kevin Lock, 7 Alan Taylor, 8 John Radford, 9 Alan Devonshire, 10 Trevor Brooking, 11 Billy Jennings.

Scorers: Alan Taylor 23, 75, Billy Jennings 34
MoM: Frank Lampard
West Ham ended the season: 17th out of 22, with 36 points.

| Number: 49 | 1976-77 | Division 1 |
| 16th May 1977 | Manchester United (h) | Att: 29,311 |

WEST HAM 4 MANCHESTER UNITED 2

If West Ham won nothing for a second year in succession after their 1975 FA Cup win, at least they could turn in a brilliant end of season run, having looked dead and buried in early March 1977. In effect, they had to beat Manchester United in their last game. Two days earlier West Ham had eked out a goalless draw at champions Liverpool. Manchester United were about to face Liverpool in the FA Cup final, but they had no intention of sending out reserves to go through the motions, or keep their best players fresh for Wembley. United could overtake Newcastle and finish fifth, so they still had something to play for.

The side Tommy Docherty put out on that Monday evening showed only keeper Alex Stepney missing, Paddy Roche taking his place. This was a season when West Ham had banned Manchester United fans, so there was more room on the terraces for home support. They were silenced when Gordon Hill put Manchester United ahead after just 25 seconds.

There is a ludicrous (apocryphal) story of Frank Lampard running over a motorcyclist on his way to this game and still going out to play, which perhaps only has resonance because of his superb equaliser.

Any team playing under the pressure of needing a win to ensure top-flight football ought to deliver if they're worthy of that place. West Ham had two such games in two years, and this one was successful. They went in level at half-time, so there was still plenty to do. West Ham quickly established a winning lead, with Pike putting them in front and 'Pop' Robson, newly returned to the club, grabbing a poacher's goal.

As has often been noted, even a two-goal cushion is soon deflated with a quick reply. Stuart Pearson, who would score the winner in that Saturday's Cup final and win a medal with West Ham three years later, hit a brilliant second for United at what would normally have been the 'away' end. Just over twenty nervous minutes remained: would West Ham hold on? Luckily, Robson hit a fine fourth seven minutes later and Hammers' fans could enjoy the remaining quarter of an hour in relative comfort.

1 Mervyn Day, 2 Billy Bonds (capt), 3 Frank Lampard, 4 Geoff Pike, 5 Tommy Taylor, 6 Mick McGivern, 7 John Radford, 8 Bryan Robson, 9 Alan Devonshire, 10 Trevor Brooking, 11 Alan Taylor.

Scorers: Frank Lampard 29, Geoff Pike 53, Bryan Robson 60, 74
MoM: Bryan Robson
West Ham ended the season: 17th out of 22, with 36 points.

| Number: 50 | 1977-78 | Division 1 |
| 8th April 1978 | Leeds United (a) | Att: 22,953 |

LEEDS 1 WEST HAM 2

1974-75 had been the first season that clubs finishing third from bottom in Divisions One and Two would go down. Three years on, having finished 18th and 17th, Hammers now ended up 20th, where they had finished in 1970-71 and, before that, in 1932-33, in Division Two. Unlike on those previous two occasions, West Ham were now relegated, back in Division Two for the first time since 1957-58.

Hammers had won 1-0 at Elland Road in extra-time in a League Cup-tie in 1971-72, and had managed a couple of recent draws there, but hadn't won there in the First Division since 1929-30. If ever they needed to break the hoodoo it was on this cold, early April Saturday.

Leeds took the lead in the 26th minute through Arthur Graham. The goal had the unusual effect of raising the Hammers to greater effort, and Alvin Martin headed in Billy Bonds' free-kick seconds before half-time.

The second half suggested a half-time rollicking, as Hammers began to run the show, looking nothing like a side in desperate relegation trouble. Eight minutes in, the bearded Derek Hales nodded in another Bonds free-kick. Leeds, however, still had a chance of European qualification, so dragged themselves back into the match. With fifteen minutes left, Leeds were awarded a penalty which dead-shot Peter Lorimer blasted wide. Hammers held on for their first top-flight win there for nearly 50 years.

Despite winning at home to Derby, and again in a 2-1 hard-fought battle at Middlesbrough, the Hammers lost 0-3 at Old Trafford and 0-2 at home to Liverpool. A draw in either game would have kept them up.

1 Bobby Ferguson, 2 Billy Bonds (capt), 3 Paul Brush, 4 Alvin Martin, 5 Tommy Taylor, 6 Bill Green, 7 Alan Curbishley, 8 Pat Holland, 9 Derek Hales, 10 Trevor Brooking, 11 Bryan Robson.

Scorers: Alvin Martin 44, Derek Hales 53
MoM: Billy Bonds
West Ham ended the season: 20th out of 22, with 32 points (relegated).

Number: 51	1979-80	League Cup QF
4th December 1979	Nottingham Forest (h)	Att: 35,856

WEST HAM 0 NOTTINGHAM FOREST 0

1977-78 was a catastrophic season, not just because of West Ham's ultimate relegation, but also thanks to two thrashing cup exits, 1-6 in the FA Cup at QPR, and 0-5 in the League Cup at Nottingham Forest. Two years later Hammers were in the Second Division and again facing Forest in the League Cup, this time in the quarter-finals, having defeated Barnsley, Southend and Sunderland to get there. To oust those three had taken seven matches, thanks to replays and a two-legged second round.

Forest had won the league title in 1978, finished second the following season, and were holders of the European Cup, not to mention defending the League Cup, which they'd won two years in succession. They were also on a 21-game unbeaten league run. For their part, relegated West Ham had finished 5th in the Second Division and currently lay 7th.

This was the team Brian Clough put out that night: Peter Shilton, Viv Anderson, Frank Gray, Ian Bowyer, Larry Lloyd, Kenny Burns, Martin O'Neill, John O'Hare, Gary Birtles, Trevor Francis, John Robertson. How many goals were Forest likely to score?

West Ham fielded the same side as for the FA Cup final the following May, although Devonshire and Pike swapped numbers, Pike wearing the hallowed '6' on this occasion. Upton Park was packed with 36,000 spectators, tickets having sold out on the first day of sale.

Peter Shilton was one reason why West Ham's Phil Parkes was not the regular England goalkeeper, and that night he was the main reason why Hammers did not reach the semi-final. First Cross and then Brooking were denied in the first half from point-blank range, the second save a reminder of that by Gordon Banks from Geoff Hurst at the same end, in the same competition, eight years previously. Alan Devonshire continually exposed weaknesses at the back of the Forest defence and provided several crosses in the second half that Cross might have converted. Devonshire himself squeezed through, but his shot sailed inches wide. Forest might have stolen the tie at the end when Trevor Francis chipped Phil Parkes, only to see his shot hit the crossbar and go out of play behind the goal.

There was no extra-time, the tie scheduled for a replay after 90 minutes stalemate, so Hammers went to the City Ground eight days later, held Forest to another 0-0, but fell 0-3 in extra-time. The game at Upton Park would not be forgotten, Hammers getting as close as they could to beating the European Cup holders.

There was, however, another domestic knock-out competition that season, and West Ham had been paired away in the third round at West Bromwich Albion of the First Division the following month.

1 Phil Parkes, 2 Ray Stewart, 3 Frank Lampard, 4 Billy Bonds, 5 Alvin Martin, 6 Geoff Pike, 7 Paul Allen, 8 Stuart Pearson, 9 David Cross, 10 Trevor Brooking, 11 Alan Devonshire, 12 P Brush.

Man of the Match: Peter Shilton
West Ham ended the season: 7th out of 22, with 47 points.

Number: 52	1979-80	FA Cup final
10th May 1980	Arsenal (Wembley)	Att: 100,000

ARSENAL 0 WEST HAM 1

The 1979-80 season saw the departures of five of West Ham's 1975 FA Cup heroes: Tommy Taylor, Mervyn Day, Billy Jennings, John McDowell and Alan Taylor. In addition, Bryan Robson, Hammers' top scorer with

26 goals the previous season, returned to Sunderland. That is some clearout. And who did John Lyall bring in to replace the sorry six? Stuart Pearson, no spring chicken. However, four games into the season, Lyall signed defender Ray Stewart from Dundee United for £400,000, and three matches later added Paul Allen from the youth team.

These changes meant the team would need time to settle, but they were needed if West Ham were to have any chance of promotion at the second attempt. They had missed out the previous season due to a poor run-in, and would do so again this season. This time it was worse, if anything, despite the same six-point margin of failure. The FA and League Cup runs could be blamed, distracting and fatiguing the team. Having said that, even today fans remember cup victories more than promotions. There wasn't the vast financial gap between the top two divisions in those days, either, which is another consideration.

To face Arsenal in an FA Cup final as underdogs from a lower division meant that the Hammers had little to lose; small wonder then that they didn't, in either sense. Arsenal were seeking a third successive victory at Wembley, but they were poor on the day, seemingly lacking spirit and drive. Their match-winner and playmaker from the previous season, Alan Sunderland, surrendered possession eight times in the first five minutes. Banners in the crowd declared 'Billy Bonds Eats Rice' and 'Devonshire Is A Delight'. The most moving sight was a Union Jack displaying the sewn-on words 'Cockney Kingdom'.

It was the 99th Cup final, and in its thirteenth minute Devonshire crosed from the left byline. David Cross's flick-on was blocked and Pearson's subsequent shot was deflected past Pat Jennings by Brooking's head. The confusion saw ITV commentator Brian Moore say: 'It went in off Brooking, I think,' and only then after viewing a couple of replays. The summariser for the day, Brian Clough, declared enigmatically: 'If he hadn't have headed it in, it would've knocked his head off, Brian.'

Alvin Martin accidentally handled a shot from Talbot in the box and Rix's effort was well saved by Parkes, but it wasn't a great first half. The heat, and the fact that neither side felt they had anything to prove, didn't help matters.

The second half saw Arsenal step on the gas but only slightly. A curler from Rix was turned round the post by Parkes, then David Price was just over on 50 minutes, and Brady hit the side netting with a left-footer on the run. Alvin Martin sustained a black eye after a clash of heads with Willie Young, before Parkes was equal to Brian Talbot's effort.

With three minutes to go, Hammers counter-attacked. Young floored Allen who was through one-on-one with Jennings. What a story it would have made, the youngest ever player in a Cup final, Paul Allen, scoring the clincher for the Hammers.

Young apologised and has since said that Allen admitted he would have done the same thing, had the situation been reversed – which Allen denies. The referee put West Ham out of their misery early, blowing after 44 minutes and 50 seconds. But Arsenal's misery was not yet complete: they then lost the European Cup-Winners' Cup final in midweek in Brussels.

As for the Cup final, its inclusion in this collection is for reasons of significance, not substance. The joy associated with Bonds lifting the Cup, and the sight of Lyall wandering around the pitch in orgiastic disbelief, makes it an occasion worth commemorating.

1 Phil Parkes, 2 Ray Stewart, 3 Frank Lampard, 4 Billy Bonds (capt), 5 Alvin Martin, 6 Alan Devonshire, 7 Paul Allen, 8 Stuart Pearson, 9 David Cross, 10 Trevor Brooking, 11 Geoff Pike, 12 Paul Brush.

Scorer: Trevor Brooking
MoM: Billy Bonds
West Ham ended the season: 7th out of 22, with 47 points.

Number: 53	1980-81	League Cup final
14th March 1981	Liverpool (Wembley)	Att: 100,000

LIVERPOOL 1 WEST HAM 1

West Ham met Liverpool twice at Wembley during 1980-81, the first being in the pre-season Charity Shield that Liverpool won 1-0 with an 18th-minute goal from Terry McDermott. The second meeting came seven months later in the Football League Cup final.

To return to Wembley less than a year after beating Arsenal was a feat, but to do so still as a Second Division side was stunning. En route to the final, Hammers had taken two First Division scalps, Tottenham and Coventry – could they take Liverpool's?

Ray Clemence was making his 32nd appearance at the Twin Towers, Phil Parkes a more humble three. How unfortunate for Parkes to have been a contemporary of Clemence and Shilton. In almost any other era, prior to Gordon Banks, Parkes would have been an automatic first choice for England. As for the other Wembley veteran, David Cross had gained a loser's medal playing for Norwich at Wembley against Spurs in 1973.

Hammers were running away with the Second Division, beaten by only three teams all season. They started well in the final, too. Alan Kennedy's foul on Jimmy Neighbour would be a straight red today. But Kennedy, as you will read, eventually had his come-uppance.

Goddard and Cross, a strike partnership that would hit 55 goals that season – 32 from Cross and 23 from Goddard – hoped for reward in the final, though Cross was well marked by Alan Hansen. Sammy Lee thought he'd put Liverpool ahead from a lay-off, but Irwin was penalised for being offside. Then Parkes saved one-handed from Dalglish's header. As half-time approached, Lampard, loitering outside the area, produced a 'special' that skidded past Clemence's far post. Goddard crossed for Devonshire's head, but Clemence saved. Liverpool were building most of their attacks on the break, whereas West Ham were more methodical, constructing opportunities from Brooking, Pike and Devonshire.

The second half saw more of the same, with a byline cross from Neighbour taken off Cross's toe by Clemence. Case replaced Heighway, making his last Wembley appearance in his retirement year. Then Parkes saved with his legs from Dalglish. Goddard found himself one on one with Clemence, but though he reached the bouncing ball first, he could not direct it over the keeper. The last chance of the 90 minutes was a header from Bonds that went wide.

Extra-time proved even more eventful. Another Neighbour cross was headed wide by Devonshire. Case hit the bar with a rocket shot that took some retrieving from the ball boys behind the goal. Cross found himself with an opportunity after Lampard had turned Brooking's ball into the area, but his header was turned over acrobatically by Clemence.

In the second period of extra-time Pearson replaced the flagging Goddard. But then it came: after panic in the Hammers' defence, Lee was grounded and Bonds ordered the defence out as left-back Alan Kennedy fired in with his right foot. The ball flew over the prostrate Lee, causing the linesman to raise his flag, but referee Clive Thomas ignored West Ham's protests and gave the goal. With just three minutes remaining it seemed desperately unjust. Further views of the incident prove that Lee was clearly interfering with play, lying on the penalty spot in an offside position. But Thomas would not be moved.

Ray Stewart reaped draconian revenge on Alan Kennedy. Although it wasn't Kennedy's fault that his controversial goal had been sanctioned, the frustrated Stewart, having being caught in a Kennedy-Hansen sandwich, chased Kennedy up the left wing and gave him an almighty kick to the shin. Kennedy, no modern diver, fell like a tree. Thomas shook his head and merely booked Stewart. Today a player could expect to be banned for the rest of the season for such a challenge. But remembering Kennedy's earlier foul on Neighbour, perhaps some kind of sad justice had been meted out.

But what about the game? As West Ham charged up the pitch in desperation, time appeared to have run out. Brooking fed Devonshire, who took the ball past two Liverpool defenders before being fouled on the edge of the area. The angry Hammer, Ray Stewart, took the kick, which he struck with venom towards the top corner until Clemence threw himself backwards to tip the ball over. West Ham pushed everyone forward for the corner. Neighbour took it and Alvin Martin powered the ball past Clemence, where the outstretched hand of Terry McDermott 'Do they do?' 'Dough they don't' tipped it onto the bar and over.

My God, a penalty to West Ham in injury-time at the end of extra-time. And who would take it? Yes, it was the angry Stewart. Bonds apparently said to him: 'Do your best – it doesn't matter if you miss – just do your best ...' Stewart said afterwards that this was what he needed to hear. Keeping his nerve, he sent Clemence the wrong way for one of the most important spot-kicks of his life. Clive Thomas blew the final whistle before Liverpool could even retrieve the ball from the net.

There followed a contretemps between Lyall and referee Thomas, following which Lyall was shown a card, but nothing could spoil the sublime spectacle the crowd had witnessed. Both sides received medals after mounting the Wembley steps – both sides got to do a lap of honour.

It was not unlike the Charity Shield game between the two sides from 1965, which had finished 2-2 (though played at Anfield). There were no penalty shoot-outs in those days. In 1981, West Ham could enjoy the drama of Stewart's penalty without having to follow it with another five (three of which they would have almost certainly missed). All they had to regret was Alan Kennedy's goal that should never have been. But then again ...

Unprejudiced fans might recall that en route to the final, in the fourth round, Hammers had beaten Norman Hunter's Barnsley with a winning goal from David Cross, 'scored' with his hands whilst lying on the ground on the goal-line! Odd that Sammy Lee was in a similar position when Alan Kennedy put the Merseysiders ahead. Churlish to complain, perhaps, but the injustice seemed more pronounced in front of 100,000 spectators at Wembley.

1 Phil Parkes, 2 Ray Stewart, 3 Frank Lampard, 4 Billy Bonds (capt), 5 Alvin Martin, 6 Alan Devonshire, 7 Jimmy Neighbour, 8 Paul Goddard, 9 David Cross, 10 Trevor Brooking, 11 Geoff Pike, 12 Stuart Pearson.

Scorers: Ray Stewart 120p
MoM: Alvin Martin
West Ham ended the season: 1st out of 22, with 66 points (champions).

| Number: 54 | 1981-82 | Division 1 |
| 2nd September 1981 | Tottenham (a) | Att: 41,200 |

TOTTENHAM 0 WEST HAM 4

Many Hammers' fans regard the 1980-81 side which won the Second Division championship as the best they have ever seen. Certainly, no Hammers side before or since amassed 66 points (with two points for a win). If there had been three points for every victory, they would have reached 94, ten more than the Boys of '86, and six more than Billy Bonds' promotion side of 1992-93. But this was a team in the Second Division – it remained to be seen whether they could cut the mustard in the big league, from which they'd been strangers for three years. The good news was that there would be more points on offer – 1981-82 was the first season offering three points for a win.

After a low-key draw at home to Brighton, Hammers faced a midweek trip across town to Tottenham, their neuro-nemesis, who they had beaten the previous season in the League Cup quarter-final, but who they hadn't faced in the league for four years since Spurs themselves were relegated from Division One.

Spurs had Hoddle and Ricky Villa in midfield, but that threat was snuffled out by Martin and Bonds, allowing Devonshire and Neighbour to terrorise the Spurs' defence. Cross opened his account with the Hammers' first serious attack, and even the Spurs fans seemed to sense this might be one of those games. Cross added a second just after half-time, the most important of the goals, after Hammers had soaked up a flood of pressure. They now gained confidence and began to counter at speed, Pike and Allen feeding off Devonshire to set up chances. Cross converted a cross from the right to complete his hat-trick on 57 minutes. West Ham were 3-0 up at White Hart Lane inside an hour, and after more Spurs pressure Cross had the cheek to add a fourth a minute from time, beating the offside trap and Clemence before the keeper could decide whether to come or stay.

The previous West Ham striker to score four away from Upton Park was ... David Cross, back in April 1981 against Grimsby Town in a 5-1 thrashing. Grimsby had at that point only conceded four goals at home all season. Cross had also scored two against Grimsby earlier in the season, in November, in a 2-1 victory at Upton Park.

1 Phil Parkes, 2 Ray Stewart, 3 Frank Lampard, 4 Billy Bonds (capt), 5 Alvin Martin, 6 Alan Devonshire, 7 Jimmy Neighbour, 8 Paul Goddard, 9 David Cross, 10 Paul Allen, 11 Geoff Pike, 12 Paul Brush.

Scorer: David Cross 10, 50, 57, 89
MoM: David Cross
West Ham ended the season: 9th out of 22 with 58 points.

| Number: 55 | 1982-83 | Division 1 |
| 11th September 1982 | Birmingham City (h) | Att: 18,754 |

WEST HAM 5 BIRMINGHAM 0

Birmingham had been strugglers in the First Division for the last few seasons, but then West Ham had only achieved a single point from their first two home games, despite a 2-0 win at Luton.

Birmingham were managed by Ron Saunders, a dour, miserable, cynical, but effective Midlands boss who had led Aston Villa to the First Division championship in 1981, but who was hardly likely to repeat that feat at Birmingham.

Billy Bonds had set a new club record four days earlier against Ipswich by making his 545th Hammers appearance, overtaking Bobby Moore's record. Frank Lampard now recorded his 500th game for the Hammers. Alan Devonshire and Alvin Martin had been named in England's squad for a European Championship qualifier against Denmark. Happy days.

Belgian import Van Der Elst opened the scoring (he would finish joint top scorer with twelve) in the 22nd minute, followed by Goddard's second of the season on the half-hour. Rather than push up to reassert themselves, Birmingham pulled men behind the ball. Thankfully England's finest (Devonshire) took them apart in the second half, putting Sandy Clark through for the penalty that Stewart converted on the hour. Alvin Martin netted a fourth – his first of the season – with a volley, and Sandy Clark bagged the fifth four minutes from time. The match programme had run a feature about Birmingham being one of West Ham's 'bogey' sides. It hasn't been run since that game.

The 5-0 thrashing was just the tonic for Lyall's men, who soon lifted themselves from eighth to second in the table, winning five games on the trot, the last two of which were a 3-2 victory at Highbury and a 3-1 thrashing of Liverpool.

1 Phil Parkes, 2 Ray Stewart, 3 Frank Lampard, 4 Billy Bonds (capt), 5 Alvin Martin, 6 Alan Devonshire, 7 Francois Van Der Elst, 8 Paul Goddard, 9 Sandy Clark, 10 Paul Allen, 11 Geoff Pike.

Scorers: Van der Elst 22, Goddard 30, Stewart 60p, Martin 73, Clark 86
MoM: Alan Devonshire
West Ham ended the season: 8th out of 22, with 64 points.

| Number: 56 | 1982-83 | Division 1 |
| 1st January 1983 | Tottenham Hotspur (h) | Att: 33,383 |

WEST HAM 3 TOTTENHAM 0

West Ham sat fifth in the First Division in their second season back, having been second two months earlier. Manager John Lyall used this New Year's Day fixture to hand a debut to seventeen-year-old Tony Cottee, and give a fourth game to fellow prodigy Alan Dickens. Spurs were in the top half, too, so this was a game to win for more reasons than usual. This might have been in the minds of ITV sports executives who picked the game to cover for *The Big Match* on Saturday night.

Spurs' star Ossie Ardiles was out with an ear infection, but they still had Glenn Hoddle, Garth Crooks, Ricky Villa and Ray Clemence in goal. Hammers were missing Brooking, Bonds, Orr, Goddard, and even Lampard with flu. Pretty much half the side, but then that's why the youngsters were playing.

Hoddle imposed himself in the opening twenty minutes, as did Van Der Elst, whose chip over Clemence almost let Cottee in, but for the intervention of O'Reilly. A free-kick on the right, taken by Hammers' captain Geoff Pike, was headed onto the crossbar by Gallagher, and with Clemence grounded, Cottee headed home. Delicious to score in your first game, but to score at the Spurs' fans end? Priceless.

Although the journey to Upton Park wasn't onerous for Tottenham, the fact that they hadn't scored in seven outings was troubling. Hoddle came closest to ending that unwanted statistic with two long shots which flew left and right of Parkes' goal. In between, Devonshire hit a fine shot from 25 yards, but this was on target and sneaking into the top corner before Clemence flapped a glove at it and sent it over the bar.

In the second half, Pike rattled Clemence's crossbar from 25 yards before Devonshire was brought down by Mazzon. Stewart struck home his fourth penalty in successive games to give Hammers a two-goal cushion. It was Stewart's tenth goal of the season (ninth from the spot) making him leading goalscorer – not bad for a right-back, even if he was playing left-back that afternoon. Ten minutes later, captain for the day Geoff Pike scored a third, Devonshire finding him with a through ball that Pike turned in.

Not just an excellent victory over an old adversary, but the beginning of a great career for Tony Cottee who would go on to score 146 goals for the Hammers in two spells, making him to date the fifth highest goalscorer ever for West Ham United.

1 Phil Parkes, 2 Ray Stewart, 3 Joe Gallagher, 4 Alan Dickens, 5 Alvin Martin, 6 Alan Devonshire, 7 Francois Van Der Elst, 8 Tony Cottee, 9 Sandy Clark, 10 Paul Allen, 11 Geoff Pike (capt), 12 Nicky Morgan.

Scorers: Cottee 25, Stewart 70p, Pike 80
MoM: Alan Devonshire
West Ham ended the season: 8th out of 22, with 64 points.

| Number: 57 | 1983-84 | League Cup R2 2L |
| 25th October 1983 | Bury (h) | Att: 33,383 |

WEST HAM 10 BURY 0

The story is legendary. Young cameraman Steve Katz has an idea – target a game with a potential hatful of goals, and offer to film it free for a share of the profits on video sales, if the result goes the right way. And this was like a major day on the tables in Las Vegas.

The net bulged for the first time on two minutes. Swindlehurst headed Walford's cross goalwards, and after two attempts, Tony Cottee tucked it away to put the Hammers 3-1 up on aggregate. It might have been very different just two minutes later when Bonds fouled Bury centre-forward Wayne Entwistle, but Bramhall's penalty came back off Phil Parkes' post. Thirteen minutes later Alvin Martin headed in Ray Stewart's free-kick at the far post. Trevor Brooking then dummied and switched feet to stroke home a third goal. Cottee then replicated his opening strike, Bonds' header going wide until Cottee appeared on the six-yard box to head the ball over the line. Four goals up, and only half an hour played.

These days, sides take their foot off the gas once they've ratcheted up a decent score, but not that night. Cottee completed a first-half hat-trick on 39 minutes, Paul Allen's early cross superbly headed in. Brooking then ghosted through the midfield before chipping Brown, only for his 25-yard effort to come back off a post.

Throughout the second half it seemed easier and easier for West Ham to find the target. A corner from Devonshire was headed goalwards by Alvin Martin and Cottee tucked away his fourth. Four minutes later Devonshire unleashed a thunderbolt into the bottom corner. When Walford was impeded in the area, Ray Stewart hit the eighth from the penalty spot, the ball going in via the same post that had denied Bury early in the first half. A free-kick from Ray Stewart was headed out to Brooking, who volleyed back in off Bury defender Bramhall, who one imagined had already suffered enough from his penalty miss. Finally, Alan Devonshire scored a tenth and his second, ghosting past Paul Hilton to play a one-two with Brooking before driving in. A record win that, thanks to the gambling prowess of Steve Katz, is preserved for posterity.

1 Phil Parkes, 2 Ray Stewart, 3 Steve Walford, 4 Billy Bonds (capt), 5 Alvin Martin, 6 Alan Devonshire, 7 Paul Allen, 8 Tony Cottee, 9 Dave Swindlehurst, 10 Trevor Brooking, 11 Geoff Pike, 12 Neil Orr.

Scorers: Cottee 2, 34, 39, 63, Martin 17, Brooking 23, 83, Devonshire 67, 81, Stewart 71p
MoM: Alan Devonshire
West Ham ended the season: 8th out of 22, with 64 points.

Number: 58	1983-84	Division 1
14th May 1984	Everton (h)	Att: 25,452

WEST HAM 0 EVERTON 1

A successful season, so why should the final game that West Ham lost be so memorable, especially as it left them 9th instead of a potential 6th? The answer is that it was Trevor Brooking's final game.

The 1983-84 season was West Ham's third back in the old First Division and was also a third successive top-ten finish for John Lyall's men. Lyall had finally built his own side to escape from the undeserved tag of being Ron Greenwood's 'assistant'. He had laid the foundations of the side that would, two seasons later, come closer than any other before or since to winning the league title. Operating with a squad of just twenty players, Lyall generated a nucleus of talent that operated as a unit rather than a bunch of individuals.

But there were still individuals, and Lyall accommodated their talents alongside the team players. One who embodied the best from an individual and also a team point of view was Trevor Brooking. Since his debut in the late 1960s, Brooking had shown his unique skills for making the brilliant look simple. A change of pace, a shimmy or twist of the body without even touching the ball and the defender would be left trailing.

Brooking probably retired a season or two prematurely, but that was his style. He wanted to quit at the top of his game, and his being Hammer of the Year in his last season makes this point. He had secured the same award in a relegation season, 1977-78, for an unprecedented third year in a row, and also in 1971-72, five times in all. To win it in a relegation year was a reward for his consistency. The fact that he stayed at the club when he could have gone elsewhere for more money made him one of a dying breed, along with Billy Bonds, Frank Lampard and Alan Devonshire.

His last appearance was irrelevant as a contest but fascinating as a spectacle. Everton's place in the FA Cup final the following weekend meant they were uninterested in a competitive challenge. But a goal from Kevin Richardson in the fourteenth minute settled the outcome.

Hammers' fans cheered Brooking every time he touched the ball, but the team were strangely subdued on the kind of floodlit occasion they often relished, and the fans were left to reflect on Brooking's skill and loyalty over the past seventeen years.

1 Phil Parkes, 2 Ray Stewart, 3 Neil Orr, 4 Billy Bonds (capt), 5 Steve Walford, 6 Warren Donald, 7 Paul Allen, 8 Tony Cottee, 9 Steve Whitton, 10 Trevor Brooking, 11 Geoff Pike, 12 Dave Swindlehurst.

MoM: Trevor Brooking
West Ham ended the season: 9th out of 22, with 60 points.

| Number: 59 | 1984-85 | Division 1 |
| 27th October 1984 | Arsenal (h) | Att: 33,218 |

WEST HAM 3 ARSENAL 1

West Ham got nine points fewer in 1984-85, which saw them slide from 9th to 16th. Norwich were relegated with 49, two fewer than West Ham.

At the end of this game, however, West Ham found themselves fifth, such had been their brilliant start to the season. They faced an Arsenal side managed by Don Howe that had also made a great start, winning five on the trot before their visit to Upton Park.

Wearing No 10 and playing in midfield, Billy Bonds threw off the years. He set up the first two goals for Cottee and Goddard, and might have had two himself before half-time. *Match of the Day* cameras were on a rare excursion to Upton Park, their interest generated by Hammers' early-season form. Goddard was a similar striker to Cottee, but could also hit the target from distance. Nevertheless, despite playing only two games fewer than Cottee that season, Goddard finished ten short of TC's final total. In this game, Arsenal pulled one back before half-time, but Pike made it safe early in the second half with a third.

What was remarkable was how West Ham overcame the Gooners more or less as they pleased, yet two games previously they had been thrashed 1-5 at Old Trafford. The sheer inconsistency of the Hammers has confounded football analysts and psychotherapists for decades. On this day it was Arsenal who were cultivating a strain of inconsistency.

1 Tom McAlister, 2 Ray Stewart, 3 Steve Walford, 4 Paul Allen, 5 Alvin Martin (capt), 6 Tony Gale, 7 Steve Whitton, 8 Paul Goddard, 9 Tony Cottee, 10 Billy Bonds, 11 Geoff Pike.

Scorers: Cottee 29, Goddard 36, Pike 49
MoM: Geoff Pike
West Ham ended the season: 16th out of 22, with 51 points.

| Number: 60 | 1984-85 | FA Cup QF |
| 9th March 1985 | Manchester United (a) | Att: 46,769 |

MANCHESTER UNITED 4 WEST HAM 2

Tom McAlister and Tony Gale joined West Ham in the season that preceded their greatest ever, which featured many performances hinting at what was to follow. The FA Cup quarter-final against Manchester United was one of those games. Despite the fact that the Hammers were beaten, they played their part and competed every bit as hard as their formidable opponents. The fact that they had even reached the last eight was due in no small part to Tony Cottee's hat-trick in the fifth round replay against Wimbledon three days earlier. In fact, he had made his FA Cup debut for West Ham against Manchester United at Old Trafford back in January 1983.

It was a remarkable performance from John Lyall's side, bearing in mind the flu epidemic that kept out Gale and Devonshire, but they started the brighter in the first twenty minutes, with Goddard, Dickens and Cottee going close, not to mention a 30-yard screamer from Neil Orr that just missed Bailey's left-hand post. It was with virtually their first attack that United scored, Mark Hughes controlling a low cross from McGrath and turning to hit a low shot past McAlister. The 5,000 travelling West Ham fans simply sang longer and louder, almost willing the equaliser. It arrived fifteen minutes later: Allen's cross deflected off Graeme Hogg's shin into the roof of the net. Moments earlier Geoff Pike had had to go off after aggravating his groin strain. He would be back at Old Trafford the following season for another FA Cup-tie, the third between the two sides in four seasons, and would score a rare header from long range.

Although West Ham deserved to take something from the game, the day belonged to Norman Whiteside. Gordon Strachan's corner was headed goalwards by McGrath, and Whiteside deflected it past McAllister. That goal before half-time took a little of the wind out of West Ham's sails. They deserved to be in front, given the chances they had created.

The second half was a different story, though almost half an hour passed before United scored their third goal. Olsen had missed two good chances, but Hogg made up for his own-goal with a free-kick to find Whiteside who slotted home. And Hammers still didn't give up, their best player, Paul Allen, cutting inside to score from a tight angle. United, however, hit a fourth three minutes later, Whiteside completing his hat-trick from the spot after Strachan had been brought down. Strachan had handed the penalty-taking duties over to Whiteside earlier in the week, and he put his first one away perfectly to complete his hat-trick.

United's absent injured captain, Bryan Robson, would return for the league fixture against the Hammers the following week in a 2-2 draw televised live by the BBC in the second half of a Terry Wogan programme, equalising soon after coming on as a substitute in the second half.

1 Tom McAlister, 2 Ray Stewart, 3 Paul Brush, 4 Steve Walford, 5 Alvin Martin (capt), 6 Alan Dickens, 7 Paul Allen, 8 Neil Orr, 9 Paul Goddard, 10 Tony Cottee, 11 Geoff Pike, 12 Paul Hilton

Scorers: Graeme Hogg 29 (own-goal), Paul Allen 85
MoM: Paul Allen
West Ham ended the season: 16th out of 22, with 51 points.

Number: 61   Season: 1985-86   Division 1
31st August 1985   Liverpool (h)   Att: 19,762

WEST HAM 2 LIVERPOOL 2

It's hard to imagine a match with Liverpool attracting under 20,000 fans, especially when these two sides would finish just four points apart in their battle for the championship. Hammers, however, had begun the season with three defeats out of four and were already in 17th position. Not the sort of form to be be in when entertaining Liverpool.

Liverpool have been, except under Graham Souness and the latter part of Gerard Houllier's reigns, a formidable side since the early 1960s. Something happens whenever Liverpool play at Upton Park. West Ham know they will have to play above themselves just to break bread, and as for beating them, the men in red will have to have a serious off day and Hammers will have to seriously fly, otherwise nowt.

On this afternoon, Liverpool arrived as runners-up to Everton in 1984-85, having been champions a year earlier. West Ham's top goalscorer Frank McAvennie (two goals), had been signed as a third striker to join Tony Cottee and Paul Goddard, gaining his place in attack with Cottee after an early-season injury to Goddard. Alan Devonshire had been back in the Hammers' side for five games, having been out since January 1984, but already looked the part, possibly even sharper than before.

Tony Cottee, scoreless since the penultimate game of the previous season, met Mark Ward's cross from the right to beat Grobbelaar at the near post but was adjudged offside. It might well have been goal of the season otherwise. No matter, West Ham were soon in front. McAvennie, chasing a flick on from Cottee, lured Grobbelaar off his line and with Hansen dithering got to the ball first. It had been raining all morning and was windy in the afternoon, but it wouldn't be the only error of the afternoon for Liverpool's erratic goalkeeper.

Liverpool barely had a look in during the first half, but as we've come to expect over the years, the red machine (actually white shirts with red shorts that afternoon) is at its most dangerous when trailing. Liverpool had completed the double over West Ham in the past two seasons but looked unlikely to repeat that on the evidence of the first 45 minutes.

Nevertheless, shortly after changing ends, Liverpool broke down the right with Phil Neal, whose low cross was turned in by makeshift striker Craig Johnston. West Ham restored their lead when Ward out on the right hit the ball to McAvennie on the corner of the six-yard box. Rushing off his line, Grobbelaar missed the ball and once again McAvennie diverted it gently into the net. All that remained was for Liverpool, who three months earlier had contested the European Cup final, to scramble a late equaliser, courtesy of Ronnie Whelan seven minutes from time. It was a harsh twist of fate for the Hammers, who should have been uncatchable. Even so, it was rare to take a point off Liverpool.

West Ham had lost 0-2 to Manchester United in the previous game, but wouldn't lose again in the league for three months.

1 Phil Parkes, 2 Ray Stewart, 3 Steve Walford, 4 Tony Gale, 5 Alvin Martin (capt), 6 Alan Devonshire, 7 Mark Ward, 8 Frank McAvennie, 9 Alan Dickens, 10 Tony Cottee, 11 Neil Orr, 12 Greg Campbell.

Scorer: Frank McAvennie 21, 71
MoM: Mark Ward
West Ham ended the season: 3rd out of 22, with 84 points (the last occasion they have ever recorded a positive goal-difference in the top flight).

| Number: 62 | 1985-86 | Division 1 |
| 29th March 1986 | Chelsea (a) | Att: 29,955 |

CHELSEA 0 WEST HAM 4

West Ham won nine of their 21 away games in 1985-86, but none gave them as much pleasure as that at Stamford Bridge. Chelsea, second in the table at New Year, were still in the top four. West Ham had just been knocked out of the FA Cup and had suffered a mini collapse, losing three in four in the league before beating Sheffield Wednesday by a McAvennie goal the previous weekend.

This victory was more exquisite by appearing on ITV's *The Big Match* that evening. Chelsea had lifted the Full Members Cup, 5-4, the previous Sunday at Wembley against Manchester City. With a hat-trick from David Speedie and two goals from Colin Lee, they must have thought they could make up ground on Everton and Liverpool, having two games in hand to recoup their four-point deficit. Striker Kerry Dixon had been dropped for the makeshift Lee. The goalmouths were mudbaths, but there was some green round the edges, from where West Ham would mount most of their attacks.

Hammers were minus captain Alvin Martin, replaced by Paul Hilton in his first game of the campaign. Chelsea tried out their third goalkeeper of the season, though there was little Steve Francis could do about

Alan Devonshire's 25-yard shot into the top corner from Tony Gale's short free-kick. It was the kind of goal that when it goes in, a team somehow knows it's going to be their day.

Hammers had looked in control on a difficult surface, not helped by pre-match and half-time downpours, and in the second half they upped the ante. Their second goal was one of the team goals of the season. Pike found Parris overlapping from left-back. A flood of racist jeers from the West Stand followed Parris up the left wing until he passed to Cottee. The diminutive striker found Dickens, who hit a precise pass into the path of Parris, who laid the ball off for Cottee to steer it past Francis.

Cottee hit his second from McAvennie's square ball, before McAvennie scored his first of the game, West Ham's fourth. Game over! On the final whistle West Ham had stolen a march on Chelsea, potentially, for the title. As a postscript, George Parris received an inscribed silver salver as Fiat Uno Young Player of the Month for March 1986.

1 Phil Parkes, 2 Ray Stewart (capt), 3 George Parris, 4 Tony Gale, 5 Paul Hilton, 6 Alan Devonshire, 7 Mark Ward, 8 Frank McAvennie, 9 Alan Dickens, 10 Tony Cottee, 11 Geoff Pike, 12 Neil Orr.

Scorers: Alan Devonshire 23, Tony Cottee 55, 64, Frank McAvennie 68
MoM: Alan Dickens
West Ham ended the season: 3rd out of 22, with 84 points.

| Number: 63 | 1985-86 | Division 1 |
| 21st April 1986 | Newcastle United (h) | Att: 24,735 |

WEST HAM 8 NEWCASTLE 1

Newcastle have a reputation for being bad travellers, and this Monday evening game was such an occasion.

In retrospect, this was a silly game between sides as mismatched as Little Red Riding Hood and the wolf. And like all bedtime stories, there was a central theme. Tonight it was 'Who wants to be in goal?' Newcastle tried Martin Thomas, Chris Hedworth and even Peter Beardsley, but hat-trick hero Alvin Martin scored against all of them. Peter Beardsley was said to have been the best of the three. Newcastle boss Iam McFaul had been thrown in at the managerial deep end, following the sudden resignation of Jack Charlton, and clearly hadn't quite got things going with his terrible Toon army.

The game was played two days after a 2-0 win at Watford, with Neil Orr in for Geoff Pike. Pike had returned from injury to play ten successive games, but had twisted knee ligaments in the 1-2 home defeat by Chelsea. He would only play ten more league games for the Hammers in his career.

By the time Orr scored his second of the season, Hammers were three up with only half an hour gone. This was four by half-time, and in the second half Alvin Martin completed an unlikely hat-trick with West Ham's eighth goal of the night. Tony Cottee must have wondered how a striker can't score when his team score eight, but it was good to see Paul Goddard, crocked from the beginning of the season, came off the bench and scored near the end.

Martin collected the ball after the final whistle, guarding it jealously as he explained he was never likely to win another. The other fact of note was future Hammers manager Glenn Roeder scoring in his own net with a volley. Years later he claimed it was 'the only way I would stop Cottee scoring'. It seemed, looking at the final list of scorers, that he was right.

1 Phil Parkes, 2 Ray Stewart, 3 George Parris, 4 Tony Gale, 5 Alvin Martin (capt), 6 Alan Devonshire, 7 Mark Ward, 8 Frank McAvennie, 9 Alan Dickens, 10 Tony Cottee, 11 Neil Orr, 12 Paul Goddard.

Scorers: Martin 3, 64p, 84, Stewart 11, Orr 35, Roeder 43 (og), Goddard 81, Frank McAvennie 83
MoM: Alvin Martin
West Ham ended the season: 3rd out of 22, with 84 points.

Number: 64   1985-86   Division 1
30th April 1986   Ipswich Town (h)   Att: 31,121

WEST HAM 2 IPSWICH 1

When Ipswich came to town for West Ham's last home fixture of the season, the crowd was 12,000 bigger than for the visit of Liverpool back in August. The two sides had endured a marathon FA Cup fourth round earlier in the year. It needed three games, the Hammers finally winning with an orange ball in the Portman Road snow in February.

This night would see another battle. Ipswich were five points above the relegation zone, so a win would bring them level with fellow strugglers Manchester City and Aston Villa. A Hammers win would lift them to second, a point behind Liverpool with two games to play. It could not have been tighter at the top or bottom. Despite his experience, it was referee Gerald Ashby's first ever game at Upton Park, and the result would hinge on a key decision late on.

Hammers had the better of a tight first half, with the headstrapped Terry Butcher marshalling his Ipswich troops. The closest Hammers came to scoring was when Ward went past two Ipswich defenders and crossed to Frank McAvennie, who headed inches wide.

As the skies darkened and the floodlights came alive, the Hammers seemed to grow in strength. Not, unfortunately, before Kevin Wilson had put Ipswich ahead midway through the second half. Stewart had lost possesion on the right as the ball skidded away from him. The subsequent long ball to Wilson evaded Martin who misjudged the bounce. Wilson's first shot came back off Parkes, but he walked the rebound into an empty net. Wilson hadn't scored for nine matches, but this goal, unchecked, would virtually insure Ipswich against the drop. Two minutes later Wilson found himself through in another one-on-one with Parkes, who blocked the shot with his upper body to give the Hammers a lifeline.

Could Hammers bounce back? McAvennie beat Butcher on the edge of the area and shot, but Paul Cooper threw up a hand and flicked the ball over the bar. Alan Dickens took a short pass from McAvennie on the edge of the area and chipped from outside the area over Cooper. Dickens hadn't scored since January and, naturally shy, his celebrations looked absurdly modest in the midst of the riotous excitement. Five minutes later, Hammers might have been pinned back again, but Jason Dozell clipped the ball over the bar from a right-wing cross.

With three minutes left, Ward was sandwiched between Brennan and Gleghorn, and although the contact seemed slight, referee Ashby pointed to the spot. Ray Stewart knew all about late penalties. He had taken two for West Ham that carried plenty of drama. His first was at Upton Park in the quarter-final of the FA Cup late in the game against Aston Villa, and he rammed that one in with ease. Then there was the penalty in the last minutes of the League Cup final against Liverpool. Again, no problem. Tonight at Upton Park, a penalty to give West Ham the lead for the first time, in a match they had to win. Stewart had scored his 50th goal from the spot two days earlier to beat Manchester City, and now hit the ball ferociously beyond Cooper.

At the press conference, Ipswich boss Bobby Ferguson let off steam at the referee, and Terry Butcher, too, had an aggressive moan in the tunnel, but Ashby's report exonerated the England defender from criticism that might have barred him from the 1986 World Cup finals in Mexico.

It was a little harsh as a penalty, but was the kind of decision you need to make a genuine attempt on the title, which the Hammers did for the first time in their history in 1985-86.

In their final two games they won 3-2 at West Brom, but then went down 1-3 at Everton, conceding second place by two points. McAvennie (28) and Cottee (26) scored 54 goals between them in a partnership that has yet to be emulated for the club. Cottee finished Hammer of the Year, and Alvin Martin went off to Mexico, as did McAvennie, appearing as substitute in two of Scotland's three Group E games.

1 Phil Parkes, 2 Ray Stewart, 3 George Parris, 4 Tony Gale, 5 Alvin Martin (capt), 6 Alan Devonshire, 7 Mark Ward, 8 Frank McAvennie, 9 Alan Dickens, 10 Tony Cottee, 11 Neil Orr, 12 Paul Goddard.

Scorers: Alan Dickens 72, Ray Stewart 86p
MoM: Alan Devonshire
West Ham ended the season: 3rd out of 22, with 84 points.

| Number: 65 | 1986-87 | Division 1 |
| 8th April 1987 | Arsenal (h) | Att: 26,174 |

WEST HAM 3 ARSENAL 1

Far from launchng a new era, that 1985-86 season turned out to be a sickeningly brief flash in the pan. The following campaign proved to be the dampest of squibs. It wasn't without its highlights, however, one of which was a 5-3 win over Chelsea. Then there was the late arrival of legendary Republic of Ireland midfielder Liam Brady, and a chance to see him playing in the English First Division again.

Brady managed twelve starts for the Hammers that season and saved his best, unsurprisingly, for the arrival of his old team Arsenal at Easter. John Lukic had denied Frank McAvennie in a 0-0 stalemate back in October 1985, but Arsenal hadn't had a great record at Upton Park over recent years. On this particular Saturday, they came to West Ham as holders of the League Cup they had won the previous week.

Tony Cottee was scoring even more prolifically than in 1985-86, but McAvennie, out for this game, had been taken out of his goal zone by a combination of desperate defences and a lack of form. In the absence of first-choice penalty taker Ray Stewart, Cottee put away an early kick, but referee Hedges awarded one at the other end eight minutes later, which

Hayes netted at the second attempt after McAlister had been penalised for moving before the kick was taken.

The second half was delayed by fighting in the South Bank which the police hadn't been able to effectively monitor. The focus descended for Arsenal fans on Stewart Robson and Liam Brady, both ex-Arsenal stalwarts, but it was Cottee who put Hammers back in the lead. Cue more crowd trouble, and Arsenal fans began to taunt Brady.

Then, a shift in the match. Brady became a man possessed by the chants that defiled him, and in the game's final throes he tortured the Arsenal defence down the left. Time after time, he would beat defenders and then retrace his steps to beat them again before firing a succession of shots in at the poor Arsenal keeper, Wilmot. He saved some of them but the others he could only watch as they flew wide of the upright or cannoned off defenders' outstretched legs.

Finally the moment arrived, and after a mazy run Brady hit a grounder, the ball curling into the bottom corner of the net. Brady could not contain himself. He ran along the chicken run and back towards the South Bank waving something at the crowd which might have been a fist, two fingers, or a small bust of George Graham. It was the seminal moment of the great Irishman's short career at Upton Park, though referee Hedges booked him for his excessive celebrations. Few Hammers fans who were there will forget the sight of Brady that afternoon, a genius midfielder in his twilight years.

1 Tom McAlister, 2 Billy Bonds, 3 Tommy McQueen, 4 Tony Gale, 5 Gary Strodder, 6 Liam Brady, 7 Mark Ward, 8 Alan Dickens, 9 George Parris, 10 Tony Cottee, 11 Stewart Robson (capt).

Scorers: Tony Cottee 4p, 56, Liam Brady 79
MoM: Liam Brady
West Ham ended the season: 15th out of 22, with 52 points.

| Number: 66 | 1987-88 | Division 1 |
| 21st November 1987 | Nottingham Forest (h) | Att: 17,216 |

WEST HAM 3 NOTTINGHAM FOREST 2

Towards the late 1980s Hammers showed only flashes of the form they had exhibited for a whole season in 1985-86, but the Lyall era was on the wane and fans had to be satisfied knowing that in a season of twenty home games, only six would be victories. Frank McAvennie left for Celtic in late September, having failed to score in nine appearances, one of which was a drab 0-0 League Cup draw at Second Division Barnsley. Even Tony Cottee, ever present this season, scored just fifteen goals, but two of these were put away in front of the England manager Bobby Robson against a team unbeaten in two months, Nottingham Forest.

Cottee's first was a dipping header over Chris Sutton from Kevin Keen's cross, snuffed out twenty minutes later by Neil Webb's neat one-two with Wilkinson. In the second half Ray Stewart stepped up to take a penalty, awarded for a foul on Cottee, with commentator Colin Benson's proclamation: 'Here's a third goal for Ray Stewart – he already has two this season.' Once the words had left his lips, Stewart hit a tame shot and saw his penalty saved. Luckily for West Ham, for Ray Stewart and commentator Benson, referee Courtney ordered a retake for encroachment. This time Stewart blasted home in a style more in keeping with his nickname 'Tonka'.

Within two minutes came the goal of the match, a stunner from Tony Cottee that he still refers to as his 'best ever goal'. A deep cross from Mark Ward dropped over the shoulders of the Forest defence and Cottee scissor-kicked the ball into the top left-hand corner. Though Nigel Clough cheered his dad with a late breakaway goal, Hammers hung on and might even have increased their lead with late efforts from Ince and Cottee.

Forest finished the season 33 points above the Hammers, which indicated the magnitude of this particular victory. Keen nabbed the man of the match ahead of Ward, mainly for his string of sublime crosses and shots that kept Hammers in front at the end. The legend that was Billy Bonds continued.

The season had its successes. Stuart Slater arrived, as did Paul Ince and a nineteen-year-old signed from Birmingham by Lyall in March 1988, Julian Dicks. Cottee would leave after six seasons, in which he scored 118 goals. The Cottee-McAvennie partnership would never return in a competitive match.

1 Tom McAlister, 2 Billy Bonds, 3 George Parris, 4 Paul Hilton, 5 Ray Stewart, 6 Kevin Keen, 7 Mark Ward, 8 Alan Dickens, 9 Paul Ince, 10 Tony Cottee, 11 Stewart Robson (capt).

Scorers: Tony Cottee 14, 52, Ray Stewart 50p
MoM: Kevin Keen
West Ham ended the season: 16th out of 21, with 42 points.

Number: 67   1987-88   Division 1
2nd May 1988   Chelsea (h)   Att: 28,521

WEST HAM 4 CHELSEA 1

Leroy Rosenior was the striker bought from Fulham for £250,000 to save John Lyall's side slipping any further. Tony Cottee was not the goalscorer he had once been, and his fifteen goals from 44 matches was nothing like Rosenior's impressive seasonal total of five goals from nine league games.

This relegation dogfight was always likely to be a game to remember, as the winner – if there was one – would surely be safe from relegation. It was one of the weakest Chelsea teams of recent years, but the lure of the fixture historically was more than enough to raise the stakes.

Rosenior hammered a loose ball into the back of Kevin Hitchcock's net, and he made it two after being put clear. A third goal from Hilton after half-time sent the crowd into raptures, though it should've been six or seven, as shots rained in from Dicks and Dickens. Substitute West grabbed a late consolation for Chelsea, though Cottee headed an even later goal to secure the thrashing.

Rosenior then sealed his bond with West Ham fans when he was sent off for fighting Chelsea's Clarke, a man who twenty years later would become coach at Upton Park. As Charlton faced Chelsea in the final game, only one of whom could escape, safety for West Ham was already assured.

Chelsea's record was now a single win in 25 games. Like West Ham, they had been title contenders a couple of years previously, but this year it was Queens Park Rangers and Wimbledon from London keeping Arsenal company in the upper reaches of the table.

Chelsea were relegated in the play-offs, which in its initial season involved the side immediately above the automatic relegation zone, plus the three clubs missing out on automatic promotion from the Second Division.

1 Tom McAlister, 2 George Parris, 3 Julian Dicks, 4 Steve Potts, 5 Paul Hilton, 6 Tony Gale, 7 Mark Ward, 8 Alan Dickens, 9 Leroy Rosenior, 10 Tony Cottee, 11 Stewart Robson (capt).

Scorers: Leroy Rosenior 14, 36, Hilton 56, Cottee 89
MoM: Stewart Robson
West Ham ended the season: 16th out of 21, with 42 points.

Number: 68   1988-89   League Cup R4
30th November 1988   Liverpool (h)   Att: 26,971

WEST HAM 4 LIVERPOOL 1

Apart from the goal he scored at Villa Park, when he ran half the pitch before hitting a dipping winner from 30 yards, this was Paul Ince's greatest moment in the West Ham shirt he couldn't wait to get off his back just six months later.

The opening goal of this League Cup-tie against mighty Liverpool was a stunning volley, because to make contact with the volley as he did, Ince had to leap off the ground, a technique he had practiced on the training ground. This time it came off spectacularly and poor Hooper had no chance at all.

Ince scored another goal three minutes later, burying Devonshire's corner-kick with a low header. Unable to believe their team were two up against the league leaders, the crowd went beserk, but Liverpool were back in it ten minutes later. A foul from Martin produced a penalty which Aldridge converted. West Ham, however, did not buckle, though it was a Liverpool player, Steve Staunton, who restored their two-goal cushion early in the second half. It followed some irresistible football from Ince and Brady preceding the cross from Kelly, which Staunton turned past his own keeper in a comic moment.

Ince almost had a hat-trick ten minutes later, only to see his low, goal-bound shot turned round the post by Hooper. Julian Dicks was then kicked in the head just outside the Liverpool penalty area. Tony Gale, not for the first time in his career, curled a beauty of a free-kick round the wall and under the crossbar to make it 4-1. Kenny Dalglish looked a small sad figure in the Upton Park dugout as he digested Liverpool's heaviest cup defeat since the war.

It turned out to be a pretty miserable relegation season for West Ham, but reaching the semi-final of the League Cup and quarter-final of the FA Cup, proved some consolation.

1 Alan McKnight, 2 Steve Potts, 3 Julian Dicks, 4 Tony Gale, 5 Alvin Martin, 6 Alan Devonshire, 7 Liam Brady, 8 David Kelly, 9 Leroy Rosenior, 10 Alan Dickens, 11 Paul Ince.

Scorers: Paul Ince 21, 24, Staunton own goal 56, Tony Gale 76
MoM: Paul Ince
West Ham ended the season: 19th out of 20, with 38 points (relegated).

Number: 69   1988-89   Division 1
22nd April 1989   Millwall (h)   Att: 16,603

WEST HAM 3 MILLWALL 0

A tiny crowd saw a giant of a result. The rivalry between these clubs dated back almost 100 years, from the days of the dockyards, and yet they met for the first time for a fixture in the league's top division and it was the Hammers who made off with the spoils.

This was the first Upton Park game after the Hillsborough disaster, preceded by a minute's silence, which some Millwall fans hijacked with a stream of obscenities. Thankfully, Hammers beat their opponents out of sight on the pitch, the first goal a shot from Julian Dicks from outside the area that Horne could not keep out. Another of Hammers' new stars, Stuart Slater, then pulled back a cross that Alan Dickens slammed home. Parris hit a third before half-time from a long ball by Dicks down the left channel. The finish was sublime.

Though Hammers laid siege to the Millwall goal, which might have led to double figures, they had to be satisfied with three. It was, however, West Ham who would be relegated come May, with Millwall finishing tenth. Hammers did, however, complete the double over Millwall, Paul Ince scoring in the 1-0 away win back in early December 1988.

1 Phil Parkes, 2 George Parris, 3 Julian Dicks (capt), 4 Tony Gale, 5 Steve Potts, 6 Alan Dickens, 7 Mark Ward, 8 Frank McAvennie, 9 Stuart Slater, 10 Kevin Keen, 11 Paul Ince, 12 Tommy McQueen.

Scorers: Julian Dicks 20, Alan Dickens 23, George Parris 43
MoM: Stuart Slater
West Ham ended the season: 19th out of 20, with 38 points (relegated).

Number: 70   1990-91   Division 2
6th October 1990   Hull City (h)   Att: 19,472

WEST HAM 7 HULL 1

Nearly 20,000 fans, now acclimatised to Second Division football, saw this game against Hull. With Billy Bonds now at the helm and Lou Macari just an oddball statistic in Hammer history, there was a sense of a return to sanity at Upton Park.

Hull hadn't lost for seven games, so might have felt they could escape Green Street with more than a drubbing. Unfortunately for them, unbeaten West Ham started positively. A move involving Bishop and Parris ended up with Jimmy Quinn slotting home left-footed. Hull hadn't gone unbeaten through slack play, however, and when Hockaday nodded on a looping cross to wrong-foot Miklosko on the half-hour, they were level.

A minute later, a rarity, a Steve Potts goal. For the record, the lucky Hammers on hand to celebrate it were George Parris and Kevin Keen, after Potts had parted the Hull defence before taking a speculative punt at goalkeeper Iain Hesford. The keeper obliged by scooping the ball into the back of the net between his legs.

Potts' cross early in the second half led to Morley being felled; Julian Dicks obliged from the spot. The fourth goal was set up for Parris after a dummy from Martin Allen, and his shot went in off the outstretched foot of a Hull defender. Next up was probably the goal of the match, Parris's overlap down the left and first-time cross was volleyed in at the far post by Quinn. Morley hit the sixth from close range after a knock-down from Quinn, and the final goal arrived after a great run from Dicks, who was fed by Morley's through ball. Dicks rounded the keeper and slotted the ball in from the narrowest of angles.

The goalfest was a welcome boost for the Hammers, who remained unbeaten in the league until Saturday, 22nd December 1990, when they fell 0-1 to Barnsley, and even then they had a 'goal' from Trevor Morley controversially ruled offside.

1 Ludek Miklosko, 2 Steve Potts, 3 Julian Dicks (capt), 4 Colin Foster, 5 Alvin Martin, 6 Kevin Keen, 7 Ian Bishop, 8 Jimmy Quinn, 9 George Parris, 10 Martin Allen, 11 Trevor Morley, 12 Frank McAvennie, 14 Matthew Rush.

Scorers: Quinn 8, 62, Potts 31, Morley 70, Dicks 46p, 81, Parris 78
MoM: Steve Potts
West Ham ended the season: 2nd out of 24, with 87 points (promoted).

Number: 71	1990-91	Division 2
11th May 1991	Notts County (h)	Att: 26,551

WEST HAM 1 NOTTS COUNTY 2

Not for the first time in their history, West Ham started the final game of the season, home to Notts County at the top of Division Two, knowing that a win would clinch the title, and give them a fantastic finish of 90 points, two in front of Oldham, even if the Latics overcame Sheffield Wednesday. County had already guaranteed their play-off place, so had little to motivate them other than retaining their winning form.

For West Ham fans, these are games to dread. You know the history, and nothing suggests it's going to be improved. Hammers had beaten Notts away 1-0 earlier in the season, thanks to one of the seventeen goals that had put Trevor Morley six ahead of Frank McAvennie in the goalscoring pecking order.

Morley was starting today, with McAvennie sub. Hammers were already promoted – neither Sheffield Wednesday nor Notts County could catch them – but Oldham had trounced them 6-0 on the Boundary Park plastic the previous season, in the semi-final of the League Cup. That needed revenge, best served cold one year on from that miserable game. West Ham had beaten Oldham at home in the league 2-0, and drawn away 1-1 just six weeks ago. Oldham had equalised two minutes from time from the spot. If Hammers had held on, it would have been all over and they'd have now been crowned champions before kick-off.

The pre-match atmosphere was best described as excitable paranoia. Within the first half-hour this proved to be amply justified, thanks to County's Mark Draper, whose two goals rendered a West Ham win unlikely.

Incredibly, Oldham were also two down in their game, the radio revelation leading to loud cheers from the West Enclosure (more radio access per capita). The difference was that the Hammers' comeback was marked by a single George Parris goal, whereas Oldham managed three to win, their third goal coming in injury-time from Neil Redfearn. In the event, West Ham's automatic promotion place was made to feel like failure, and the post-match lap of honour was flat.

At least Notts County weren't just party poopers; they retained their form into the play-offs and eventually joined West Ham and Oldham on a trip into the First Division at the end of the season.

1 Ludek Miklosko, 2 Steve Potts, 3 George Parris, 4 Tim Breacker, 5 Colin Foster, 6 Chris Hughton, 7 Ian Bishop (capt), 8 Stuart Slater, 9 Iain Dowie, 10 Martin Allen, 11 Trevor Morley, 12 Frank McAvennie, 14 Kevin Keen.

Scorer: George Parris 77
MoM: Martin Allen
West Ham ended the season: 2nd out of 24, with 87 points (promoted).

Number: 72   1991-92   Division 1
22nd April 1992   Manchester United (h)   Att: 24,197

WEST HAM 1 MANCHESTER UNITED 0

West Ham's return to the top flight after a two-year absence was a bit like sending your four-year-old off to start school a year too early. Hammers' fans watched their side waddle confidently into the playground, but just when it looked like they might be there to stay, the wobble came, and they fell down. After their 0-2 reverse at home to Crystal Palace on 20th April, Hammers were relegated. Ignominy. Three games to go and nothing to fight for. And what made it worse was that the party poopers from a year earlier, Notts County, were down there with them, ready for a swift return to the kick and rush (and yet more kicking) of the Second Division.

Just the right time, then, to face Alex Ferguson's leaders Manchester United. Against their juggernaut players, West Ham sported the likes of Mitchell Thomas and the sadly fading 'top scorer' Mike Small, and even had a substitute debutant called Dean Martin, suggesting the phrase 'Old Claret Eyes is Back'.

Early in the season, Ken Brown's son Kenny had hit a spectacular late goal from 25 yards in a 3-1 home win over Aston Villa. He would achieve something even more memorable in this game, which was meant to see Manchester United close in on their first title for 25 years.

All Ferguson's men managed to do for the first three-quarters of the game was hover around Miklosko's penalty area. They did not muster a single first-half shot on goal. Twenty minutes into the second half, a weak Pallister clearance ran into the path of the oncoming Kenny Brown who hit a screamer into the left-hand corner of Schmeichel's goal. To this day, some say that the power came from Pallister's clearance striking the West Ham defender's shin, but the shot appeared intentional.

Thereafter United stepped up a gear but could find no inspiration or opportunity in the remaining 25 minutes. Afterwards, Alex Ferguson memorably described West Ham's 'effort' during the game as 'obscene'.

1 Ludek Miklosko, 2 Steve Potts, 3 Julian Dicks (capt), 4 Tony Gale, 5 Alvin Martin, 6 Mitchell Thomas, 7 Ian Bishop, 8 Kevin Keen, 9 Mike Small, 10 Kenny Brown, 11 Stuart Slater.

Scorer: Kenny Brown 66
MoM: Julian Dicks
West Ham ended the season: 22nd out of 22, with 38 points (relegated).

Number: 73   1991-92   Division 1
2nd May 1992   Nottingham Forest (h)   Att: 20,629

WEST HAM 3 NOTTINGHAM FOREST 0

West Ham's victory over Manchester United wasn't as unexpected as the press reports might have suggested, but what happened in the final game, just over a week later, was pure football theatre.

Frank McAvennie. A one-season wonder at Upton Park some might say, and there have been a few of those at the club, but the broken leg at Stoke in the opening game of 1989-90 had hardly helped rid McAvennie of that sobriquet in his second stint at the Boleyn. However, he was about to leave West Ham for pastures new, as was clear from his being named among the substitutes for the final game, against Brian Clough's Forest, as he had been against Notts County a year earlier.

With nothing to play for, West Ham or McAvennie, the excitement-starved crowd were treated to probably West Ham's finest performance of the season. Stripped of their stress, Billy Bonds men knocked the ball around with confidence in the first half.

Even Bonds tired of the terminally underachieving Mitchell Thomas at half-time and decided he might as well give the departing McAvennie a 45-minute run-out. McAvennie went on to hit three goals in 25 minutes, the best of which was the last. The ball went from Dicks to Bishop to McAvennie, who held off a defender before steering it past Forest keeper Crossley.

There was a moment after that third goal when the clock seemed to flash back to goals scored six years earlier in the Great Season, and the North Bank called and sang Frank's name loud and long. The passing of a legend on the eve of a desperately disappointing low point, culminating in the wooden spoon. Suffered in May 1978, May 1989 and now May 1992, no football fan forgets such misery when their team falls from the top league. McAvennie, with his flash of a brilliant career passing, somehow made that pain a little easier to bear.

1 Ludek Miklosko, 2 Steve Potts, 3 Julian Dicks (capt), 4 Tony Gale, 5 Alvin Martin, 6 Mitchell Thomas, 7 Ian Bishop, 8 Martin Allen, 9 Mike Small, 10 Dean Martin, 11 Stuart Slater, 12 Frank McAvennie.

Scorer: Frank McAvennie 60, 81, 85
MoM: Frank McAvennie
West Ham ended the season: 22/22 with 38 points (relegated).

Number: 74   1992-93   Division 1
21st November 1992   Oxford United (h)   Att: 11,842

WEST HAM 5 OXFORD 3

West Ham's immediate return to the Second Division was bad enough. But what was this? They were still in the First Division. Except it was full of teams with names like Brentford and Southend United. Brentford in the First Division – were we back in the 1940s? But this was just the latest ludicrous football ploy to gentrify the game. The old First Division was the new Premier League, and the old Second Division was the new First Division. So that's all right then.

Provided West Ham could escape from the new First Division as quickly as possible, yes that would be fine, thanks. And taking another step in that direction was the overturning of Oxford. The Hammers were fired up by Julian Dicks returning from a five-match ban, during which they had lost three games and won only one. He must have saved up plenty of fire-power as he scored two stunning long-range shots that set Upton Park alight. They came either side of half-time, both from well-worked free-kicks.

Beforehand, Hammers had built up a lead through Clive Allen and Tim Breacker, replying to John Durnin's opening Oxford goal in the first minute. West Ham were well served by the industry of young midfielder Mark Robson, the first new Robson since the departure of Keith and Bryan in the late 1970s. The outcome had seemed comfortable for the Hammers until goals from Magilton and Melville brought Oxford sensationally back to 3-4, but a very late finish from Trevor Morley gave Hammers breathing space.

One of the stars of the young Oxford United team that afternoon was Joey Beauchamp (pronounced 'Beecham'). Billy Bonds made a note to enquire about his tenure later in the season. It would be the beginning of a farcical 'non-transfer' saga that would indirectly lead to Bonds' departure from the club for good.

1 Ludek Miklosko, 2 Tim Breacker, 3 Julian Dicks (capt), 4 Steve Potts, 5 Alvin Martin, 6 George Parris, 7 Mark Robson, 8 Mattie Holmes, 9 Trevor Morley, 10 Clive Allen, 11 Kevin Keen, 12 Kenny Brown.

Scorers: Allen 4, Breacker 38, Dicks 42, 50, Morley 86
MoM: Julian Dicks
West Ham ended the season: 2nd out of 24, with 88 points (promoted).

Number: 75   1992-93   Division 1
8th May 1993   Cambridge United (h)   Att: 27,399

WEST HAM 2 CAMBRIDGE UNITED 0

If Frank McAvennie was a one-season wonder, what does that make David Speedie? The history books will chronicle his Hammers' career as that of an ex-Chelsea striker who put on a West Ham shirt eleven times and scored four goals. But the truth is more complex than that.

Billy Bonds knew from his experience as a player that if you don't bounce back from relegation immediately you might be stuck in the second level for some time to come. You would 'forget' how to play football in the top league. At the business end of a season that saw a much closer finish than the previous promotion season of two years earlier, West Ham finished strongly. They beat Birmingham with two goals in the last three minutes, after trailing for most of the game. Then David Speedie, a late March signing, scored twice in his sixth game, against Leicester, and still the fans were slow to warm to him. Luton beat Hammers with two goals in the last five minutes, before three wins set up a last-match date with destiny, not unlike that against Notts County in May 1991. On this afternoon, however, West Ham were not guaranteed automatic promotion. Portsmouth, who had been breathing down their neck all season, could overtake them if Hammers stumbled at home against Cambridge, who had to win themselves to stay up. A footballing drama of the first order. And it couldn't have been more dramatic.

With the goal-difference tight, the calculations were these: Newcastle were already guaranteed the championship. Portsmouth had to beat Grimsby by more than West Ham beat Cambridge to claim the second automatic promotion place. Grimsby, however, were in the upper reaches of the table and had nothing to play for.

So to return to David Speedie, who had scored in Hammers' 3-1 win over Bristol Rovers two matches previously. Now, on this vital Saturday afternoon, he scored a minute after half-time to finally give Hammers a lead. Portsmouth were already beating Grimsby 2-1. Then the turning point: Cambridge broke out of the siege to their goal and Leadbitter slipped a superb equaliser. Would it be enough to keep them up? No, it wouldn't – the linesman's flag was raised high in front of the chicken run for offside.

In the final seconds, with home supporters over the hoardings and hovering dangerously close to the pitch, Hammers broke one more time down the left. Julian Dicks went on a mazy run that saw him tearing down on keeper Filan. Rather than risk him making a hero of himself, Dicks looked up and saw substitute Clive Allen lurking at the far post in front of an open goal, so he squared the ball and Allen gleefully slid it in. Pitch invasion. Pandemonium.

Bonds had managed two promotions in three years, something no Hammers' manager had achieved previously.

1 Ludek Miklosko, 2 Tim Breacker, 3 Julian Dicks (capt), 4 Steve Potts, 5 Tony Gale, 6 Ian Bishop, 7 Mark Robson, 8 Peter Butler, 9 David Speedie, 10 Trevor Morley, 11 Kevin Keen, 12 Clive Allen, 14 Martin Allen.

Scorers: David Speedie 47, Clive Allen 90
MoM: Steve Potts
West Ham ended the season: 2nd out of 22, with 88 points (promoted).

Number: 76	1993-94	Premiership
18th September 1993	Blackburn Rovers (a)	Att: 14,437

BLACKBURN 0 WEST HAM 2

Back in the top division, or whatever anyone might call it, Billy Bonds' West Ham were wobbling in the playground again. Seven games played, one victory, two draws and four defeats, and bottom of the new Premier League. Great.

For a team that would win the Premiership the following season, Blackburn weren't enjoying boom attendances. Just over 14,000 would turn up to watch this game.

One of the redeeming factors about the Hammers over the years has been their ability to extract another season or two from warhorse strikers out to pasture. Not that Lee Chapman was exactly such. He had been a title winner in 1992 with Howard Wilkinson's Leeds. Hammers, though, hadn't scored in 270 minutes' action, so something had to give. Thankfully, on this afternoon, it was Rovers' defence. Bonds had decided with Graeme Souness that Hammers captain Julian Dicks could leave for Liverpool in a straight swap for defender David Burrows and midfield dynamo Mike Marsh. Chapman had rejected a move to Hammers to join Portsmouth six weeks earlier, but had a rethink and went straight into Bonds' scarily new-look team. Would the new signings reverse the club's slide in the new league?

Hammers began promisingly and might have had a couple of goals on the half hour. Marsh in particular showed pace and timing in his passes, and proved a useful foil for Bishop. Ludek Miklosko saved well from Warhurst before Dale Gordon set up Chapman, who nipped between Berg and Mimms to walk the ball into the empty net. It was one of those opportunities that on most days might have bounced less favourably, but a bit of good luck on this occasion made all the difference.

After half-time Miklosko made fine saves from Wilcox and Newell. Blackburn, under Kenny Dalglish and with Jack Walker's money, clearly had the Premier League title on their shopping list. They had already seen Miklosko's talents, unaware of what was to come and how much they would be grateful for them on a May afternoon in 1995.

As for today, Hammers hadn't quite finished the job. Left-back turned right-back Keith Rowland found himself by the right corner flag, from where his cross was turned past Mimms by Trevor Morley's diving header. Rowland and Gordon, both playing their first matches of the season, had combined with the other new boys to fashion a memorable 2-0 away win that had kick-started Hammers' first season in the Premiership.

1 Ludek Miklosko, 23 Keith Rowland, 33 David Burrows, 4 Steve Potts (capt), 12 Tony Gale, 14 Ian Bishop, 11 Dale Gordon, 16 Mattie Holmes, 25 Lee Chapman, 34 Mike Marsh, 9 Trevor Morley, 6 Martin Allen.

Scorers: Lee Chapman 33, Trevor Morley 71
MoM: Ludek Miklosko
West Ham ended the season: 13th out of 22, with 52 points.

Number: 77	1993-94	Premiership
4th April 1994	Tottenham Hotspur (a)	Att: 31,502

TOTTENHAM 1 WEST HAM 4

A Saturday afternoon at White Hart Lane invariably induces an excited dread in the stomach. Should it end in defeat, it will be like losing two games on the same day because Spurs fans are the nemesis for West Ham purists who know football.

This season Hammers faced a Tottenham side which had only won three times at home in eighteen games. Sadly, that was usually the sort of time when Hammers would spark Spurs back to form with an inept display. Does it always have to be that way?

Peter Butler's first-half injury was the turning point, introducing substitute Steve Jones. The long-legged occasional Hammer took Bishop's through ball in his stride and bashed it into the net.

In the second half, Spurs offered an entry for the most unnecessary penalty of the season. Kevin Scott climbed over Morley and the West Ham striker lofted the spot-kick past Ian Walker. Bizarrely, Morley found himself in his own area six minutes later, tackling Mabbutt's leg rather than the ball, and substitute Sheringham spot-kicked home. Morley managed a goal from open play next, from an acute angle, the Spurs' commentator barely hiding his partisan frustration in the commentary. West Ham's fourth, ten minutes from time, was a lovely extended one-two between Marsh and Holmes, Marsh finishing with a neatly placed shot from Holmes' weighted return.

Despite Spurs' pants season, it was a Hammers victory to savour.

1 Ludek Miklosko, 2 Tim Breacker, 23 Keith Rowland, 4 Steve Potts (capt), 5 Tony Gale, 14 Ian Bishop, 8 Peter Butler, 28 Matthew Rush, 9 Trevor Morley, 34 Mike Marsh, 16 Mattie Holmes, 17 Steve Jones.

Scorers: Steve Jones 37, Trevor Morley 60p, 72, Mike Marsh 80
MoM: Mattie Holmes
West Ham ended the season: 13th out of 22, with 52 points.

Number: 78	1994-95	Premiership
17th December 1994	Manchester City (h)	Att: 17,286

WEST HAM 3 MANCHESTER CITY 0

1994-95 was the season when the Hammers welcomed back two of their greats from Merseyside, from Everton Tony Cottee and from Liverpool Julian Dicks. It was also the season when Harry Redknapp stepped into the breach following the speedy and mysterious departure of Billy Bonds.

Dicks had always been a sore for Bonds. Now with Redknapp, he was clearly a changed man – part of which must have been due to his time in a very different set-up at Anfield. Once Souness had left, Dicks had to deal with Roy Evans, who had no time for the antics of the mercurial defender. Cottee had also cultivated a personality clash with Everton boss Mike Walker, and despite scoring 99 goals and finishing top scorer every season but one, 'TC' was seeing too much of the subs' bench to think that his future lay with the Toffees.

Both players returned to Upton Park and were soon in the first team as if they had never left. All that had changed was a little pace and Dicks' temperament, its Neanderthal veneer expertly t-cutted, possibly as a result of becoming a father, amongst other things.

This was Cottee's game. He had bagged plenty of hat-tricks and registered an astonishing six for Everton in five seasons, but had yet to score three in a home fixture in the league for West Ham.

On a cold evening in mid-December, Cottee set about the Manchester City defence, controlling a high ball with one touch, and hammering the ball left-footed at Andy Dibble with the second. The keeper beat it out, only to find Cottee ramming it past him with his right. A goal in six minutes and another came three minutes later, after a penetrating run from Tim Breacker. Cottee swivelled past a defender and wrong-footed the keeper with a flick of the right foot.

West Ham had to wait almost 50 minutes for the final goal, probably the best of the three. Tireless Ian Bishop put Cottee away on the right. He swerved past his marker and volleyed left-footed past Dibble.

Cottee would only enjoy one more full season at Upton Park.

1 Ludek Miklosko, 2 Tim Breacker, 3 Julian Dicks (capt), 4 Steve Potts, 5 Alvin Martin, 11 Mattie Holmes, 7 Ian Bishop, 17 Michael Hughes, 14 Matthew Rush, 25 Jeroen Boere, 27 Tony Cottee.

West Ham's scorer: Tony Cottee 6, 9, 57
MoM: Tony Cottee
West Ham ended the season: 14th out of 22, with 50 points.

Number: 79	1994-95	Premiership
14th May 1995	Manchester United (h)	Att: 24,783

WEST HAM 1 MANCHESTER UNITED 1

I make no apology for selecting Manchester United nine times in these 101 games. Their contests against the Irons over the years have run from sublime to supreme examples of how football should be played.

In a special evening at Upton Park in May 2008 to celebrate Ron Greenwood and John Lyall's achievements, guest of honour Sir Alex Ferguson had this to say: 'I think West Ham are a fantastic football club and the philosophy of the football club has been fantastic for a long, long time.' Thanks, Sir Alex. You're right of course.

If you'd caught the Manchester United boss late on this day in May 1995, he might not have been so gushing. For West Ham it was another perfect time to face the perennial First Division title hunters. United were then, on the last day of the season, two points behind Blackburn who led the table and were playing at Liverpool. Liverpool wanted fourth place, which required a win; Dalglish's Rovers would love to clinch the title at Anfield. However, if Rovers lost, Manchester United could leapfrog them with a win at Upton Park. Hammers had beaten Liverpool 3-0 four days earlier to erase any faint chance of relgation, so were in good spirits. Dicks, however, was injured, so it was a relief that Hammers did not need anything from the game. That sense of freedom would inspire them on this tense last day.

A canopy of Carling lager cans was stashed in the small hallway next to the tunnel, along with a replica Premiership trophy, in case Manchester United were to win it. It was an inverted compliment to the Hammers that the real trophy had gone to Anfield, as Blackburn were the most likely champions. But no one could have guessed how things would shape at Upton Park that afternoon.

West Ham were clearly the more relaxed, stringing passes together and creating early chances. 'Mattie' Holmes, as he had dubbed himself recently, was industrious and dangerous, and with John Moncur lurking on the left of the penalty area, United slowed to take stock of the threat. It was during one of these unnaturally cautious Man U periods that West Ham scored, Holmes' drive and Michael Hughes' knack of being in the right place at the right time contributing to a half-time lead.

United cranked it up in the second half, laying siege to Miklosko's goal at the South Bank end. Time after time they were thwarted by ranks of Hammers defenders. If they got past those they had to face Miklosko. The giant Czech, shot-stopper supreme, threw himself at everything. Eventually Brian McClair converted another opportunity, and United were level. Now they needed a winner.

Shots from Andy Cole, headers from McClair and Sharpe, and crosses and chips from Paul Ince. How Judas would have loved a title win at the Boleyn. Somehow, Hammers held on. United fans, who had cheered West Ham's unexpected 2-0 home victory over Blackburn in April, began to mutter as full-time approached. Then news that Liverpool, who had been drawing 1-1 with Blackburn, had scored in the last minute. United only needed to score themselves to claim the Premier League. But they could not and they did not.

Hammers' subdued lap of 'honour' for avoiding relegation must have looked like mockery to United's stars watching from the touchline. But the Blackburn fans would not forget this moment, and Miklosko received a standing ovation on his next appearance at Ewood Park in December.

1 Ludek Miklosko, 2 Tim Breacker, 12 Keith Rowland, 4 Steve Potts (capt), 8 Marc Rieper, 10 John Moncur, 7 Ian Bishop, 17 Michael Hughes, 26 Don Hutchison, 9 Trevor Morley, 11 Mattie Holmes, 6 Martin Allen, 18 Simon Webster.

Scorer: Michael Hughes 31
MoM: Ludek Miklosko
West Ham ended the season: 14th out of 22, with 50 points.

Number: 80	1995-96	Premiership
31st January 1996	Coventry City (h)	Att: 18,884

WEST HAM 3 COVENTRY CITY 2

This was an improved season, which gave the Hammers their first top-half finish since that magical third place ten years previously. It was also the first serious blooding of youth since the Boys of '86 generation, for waiting in the wings were Lampard Jnr and Rio Ferdinand, not to mention a horde of foreigners arriving to grab the next few seasons' headlines at Upton Park.

The stadium had been fitted with two new giant replay screens which gave the crowd the chance to relive the action (strictly West Ham goals and non-controversial incidents). The first half required virtually no replays, but the second was a different story. Indeed it was a 'foreigner', tall Danish defender Marc Rieper, who'd joined the club a year earlier, who put the Hammers in the lead just after half-time. He slammed in a shot after first Cottee and then Bishop had failed to make contact in front of Ogrizovic's goal. Another Hughes' corner led to a further chance for Rieper, but his header flew off the post.

West Ham were playing neat, incisive one-touch football, spraying passes around. When Dicks found Bishop, he hit a weighted ball through to Cottee who took on Ogrizovic and Shaw, and beat them both to register a second for the Hammers. With three recorded angles on the goal, and a flick or two of the replay machine, spectators were able to enjoy the goal three times more before Coventry could kick off.

Coventry put together neat moves themselves, one of which ended up with Dion Dublin bundling the ball over the line at the far post.

Then came an intriguing double substitution; two No 26s: for West Ham, Frank Lampard junior, ready to debut, and for Ron Atkinson's Coventry, Gordon Strachan, in his last season as a player, old enough to be young Frank's dad. Harry Redknapp put his arms round both to wish them luck as they came on. Strachan was the first to make his presence felt, contributing to the build up that concluded with Noel Whelan's fine finish. Coventry were level thirteen minutes after going 0-2 down.

Step up an unlikely match winner. Iain Dowie in his second stint at West Ham, was lurking behind the Coventry defence as Williamson sliced an overhead kick goalwards from the edge of the area. Dowie shoved past Shaw to slide the ball beyond Ogrizovic.

West Ham held on confidently to sneak the game 3-2. That was particularly satisfying for Frank Lampard junior, and for his dad Frank senior, the assistant manager under Harry Redknapp.

1 Ludek Miklosko, 15 Kenny Brown, 3 Julian Dicks (capt), 4 Steve Potts, 8 Marc Rieper, 7 Ian Bishop, 10 John Moncur, 14 Iain Dowie, 9 Tony Cottee, 20 Danny Williamson, 24 Michael Hughes, 22 Adrian Whitbread, 26 Frank Lampard Jnr.

Scorers: Marc Rieper 46, Tony Cottee 59, Iain Dowie 85
MoM: Danny Williamson
West Ham ended the season: 10th out of 20, with 51 points.

Number: 81   1995-96   Premiership
23rd March 1996   Manchester City (h)   Att: 24,017

WEST HAM 4 MANCHESTER CITY 2

Another game against Manchester City, soon to be relegated. And what a
game! Memorable for sublimely executed goals, a penalty save, avenging
a New Year's Day defeat at Maine Road, and Iain Dowie scoring, yet
again. He actually scored one third of his goals this season against the
same team. This was also a game dominated by events involving Irish
internationals, Northern and Southern.

In his time as West Ham manager, Harry Redknapp exhausted the
term 'maverick' with signings predicated on a combination of hope and
desperation. Harry took risks that would have baffled even amateur psy-
chologists. He suggested in the days before the match that City to be relegated at 6-1 was the best bet around, something which didn't please the
City boss Alan Ball, but which turned out to be a top-drawer tip. This was
a game that had Dumitrescu, Bilic, Rieper and substitute Dani represent-
ing the Rest of Europe in West Ham's colours – Rieper's West Ham
appearances more than doubling those of the other three – but in spite
of this, it was a curiously English game.

Hammers lay 11th from mid-February to late April, but squeezed
above Chelsea to 10th on the last day. This afternoon, however, they were
in classic 'run and bluster' mode. Dowie's opener was a powerful header
after a nod-on from fellow Northern Ireland international Michael
Hughes, and West Ham somehow carried their lead to the interval. There
were two reasons for this, one being the profligacy of City striker Uwe
Rosler (another from the Rest of Europe squad) and the other being their
captain Keith Curle. After Kinkladze had been upended by Northern
Ireland international Keith Rowland, Curle's penalty towards the bottom
left-hand corner was easily saved by Miklosko He waved away the con-
gratulations from teammates like irritating flies.

The second half saw the expulsion of another Northern Ireland international, City's irascible, red-haired Steve Lomas – who would join the
Hammers within a year – for a second bookable offence. It was clearly
not a day to be a travelling City supporter. Shortly afterwards, Dowie
thumped another header into the net, his curiously bestial appearance
contrasting exquisitely with the tanned and chiselled features of West
Ham's beautiful Portuguese substitute, Dani. As with Dowie's first goal,
the chance was created by Michael Hughes, this time with an inswinging
corner. At the other end, the only other Premiership striker of Dowie's

aerial command, Eire forward Niall Quinn, made his mark with a goal twenty minutes later. Miklosko dropped substitute Hiley's cross in the mud. The ball died at the feet of Quinn, who tapped in.

Two-goal Dowie had played under Alan Ball at Southampton earlier in his career, but manager and player fell out, so revenge in a West Ham shirt was in Dowie's top pocket.

Following Quinn's reply for City, there followed two of the best West Ham goals of the season. Foraging out on the right, Hughes hit a cross-field pass to Dicks, who hit a rising torpedo of a shot from 30 yards. Within a minute, Dani broke free on the right, teasing his pursuers before pushing the ball beyond Immel. The ensuing celebrations saw Dani hugged by Dowie and Dicks in what could be described as a beauty-and-beasts human sandwich.

In injury-time Quinn took another pass from Hiley and hit a rocket past Miklosko. The goal prompted the final whistle from referee Cooper, and Quinn took a series of gentlemanly handshakes from his Irish colleagues on both sides as the teams left the field.

1 Ludek Miklosko, 2 Tim Breacker, 3 Julian Dicks (capt), 28 Slaven Bilic, 8 Marc Rieper, 7 Ian Bishop, 24 Michael Hughes, 14 Iain Dowie, 18 Ilie Dumitrescu, 20 Danny Williamson, 12 Keith Rowland, 16 Dani.

Scorers: Iain Dowie 21, 51, Julian Dicks 83, Dani 84
MoM: Michael Hughes
West Ham ended the season: 10th out of 20, with 51 points.

Number: 82   Season: 1996-97   Premiership
24th February 1997   Tottenham Hotspur (h)   Att: 24,017

WEST HAM 4 TOTTENHAM 3

Eric Morecambe once asked why English batsmen were so scared of the female Australian bowler Lillian Thompson. If he'd still been around he might have raised eyebrows at Hammers' 1996-97 saviour, Kitson-Ann Hartson. She scored thirteen goals, and in this game made her home debut, scoring twice.

The game was played in wind, rain and murk, having been put back to Monday thanks to Sky Sports' scheduling. By then, West Ham knew that it was even more of a 'must win' game, other teams around the relegation zone having picked up points on the Saturday. Hammers were 17th, which was bad enough. But for Forest's grim form and Middlesbrough being deducted three points, West Ham would have been in the bottom three. The tenth place of the previous season, Redknapp's best, looked to have been a flash in the pan. A sheath of highly paid foreign players had left, and although Bilic had settled in defence, the strikeforce looked pretty feeble. Dowie had exhausted teams and managers for payback, Tony Cottee had left for a king's ransom in Malaysia, and hopes that 'two bob' Romanian star Florin Raducioiu would reproduce his international form at Upton Park was long since sacrificed on the perfume counters of Harvey Nichols. Defeat in the FA Cup by Third Division Wrexham had been a further warning of troubles ahead.

Redknapp temporarily abandoned his legion of foreign starlets in favour of an old-fashioned, established British bruiser, John Hartson, and a more svelt and light-footed sidekick, Paul Kitson. The £7 million outlay looked excessive in the light of a 0-1 defeat at Derby, where both made their debuts, but the visit of Spurs would allow the duo to make an early impression on home fans.

The wind was clearly going to affect play, and it did. After eight minutes Sheringham turned Carr's cross, intended for Iversen, into the opposite corner of Miklosko's net. The Spurs bench punched their arms into the rain, even the terminally sedentary Gerry Francis.

Relishing his role as captain, Julian Dicks set about doing something even the great Michael Fish had failed to do: take control of the weather. Two prodigious throws into the Spurs' penalty box hung like bombs on parachutes, the second put behind for a corner by Sol Campbell under pressure from Hartson. Michael Hughes whipped the ball over to Dicks, who headed firmly into the right-hand corner of the net.

Conceding possession from the restart, Tottenham chased back as Hammers broke again. Kitson put Hughes through, only for his snapshot to be finger-tipped over by Walker. As Walker came for Hughes' corner, the ball dropped onto the head of Kitson, who threw himself to nod West Ham into the lead. Two goals in less than a minute!

Darren Anderton proved five minutes later that he, too, could twist the conditions to his own end, though not as he intended. Iversen flicked the ball to him, and Anderton chipped the ball over a stranded Miklosko, but a good four feet wide. Or that was where it was going until a gust of wind corrected the schoolboy miss and turned the effort goalwards. Even then it might have sailed over the bar, but the wind killed the bounce and carried the ball into the net. The FA, in that week's dodgy goals meeting, should have credited the goal to William Wind. As it was, Tottenham were level.

Anderton conceded a free-kick shortly after, bundling over Dicks near halfway. Dicks took the kick himself, the ball dropping towards Hartson, who headed in at the far post. A hat-trick of West Ham headers, and the lead regained.

The second half was no less frenetic. Spurs had the first say, Howells bringing them level after 53 minutes, almost passing Sheringham's back-flick into the corner of the net. Then, the telling moment of the match, as Kitson flicked on Breacker's free-kick to Hartson, who was upended by Howells. Dicks hit the penalty with such ferocity that it would have beaten three keepers on the line, let alone Walker. 4-3.

This was only West Ham's second win in five months of Premiership football, but it sparked some fine form and an escape from relegation by two points. Kitson ended up with eight goals, and Hartson five. Kitson was top goalscorer, equal with captain Dicks, who also finished the sea-son with another deserved fans' Hammer of the Year award.

1 Ludek Miklosko, 2 Tim Breacker, 3 Julian Dicks (capt), 27 Rio Ferdinand, 4 Steve Potts, 20 Mark Bowen, 24 Michael Hughes, 7 Ian Bishop, 16 John Moncur, 10 John Hartson, 9 Paul Kitson, 14 Iain Dowie.

Scorers: Julian Dicks 21, 72p, Paul Kitson 22, John Hartson 38
MoM: Julian Dicks
West Ham ended the season: 14th out of 20, with 42 points.

Number: 83	1997-98	Premiership
27th September 1997	Liverpool (h)	Att: 25,908

WEST HAM 2 LIVERPOOL 1

Victories over Liverpool over the years have achieved mythical status, no matter how they are won, so when the game is memorable for its quality, it's guaranteed to be one that no one will forget.

Harry Redknapp had come within a whisker of losing his job in 1996-97. As with most aspects of football life, necessity can often prove the stepmother of invention, and so it proved in this case. Recognising that he had goalscorers, but perhaps not goalmakers, Redknapp signed Southampton's Eyal Berkovic, the 'vic' pronounced 'vits' by the com-mentating fraternity. Berkovic had scored against Spurs, who had been pipped for his services by the Hammers, therefore giving everyone in the claret and blue camp an early shot of sporting one-upmanship joy.

Against Liverpool the following month, Berkovic was put through by Iain Dowie and he beat the advancing David James with the speed if not the power of his shot. The ball struck the inside of the post but fell into the path of Hartson, who swept it into the net. New signing Andy Impey had his fierce shot tipped over by James. Hammers were on fire.

This game offered another chance to boo the returning Paul Ince, resplendent in the cowardly yellow of Liverpool, appropriate given the many years Ince had failed to show whenever given the chance to play at Upton Park. Robbie Fowler equalised for Liverpool just after half-time with a left-foot volley, but Berkovic, despite never smiling once in 79 games for the Hammers, had the last laugh, with a right-foot shot from the edge of the area, after Hartson's flick on had flat-footed the Liverpool defence. This was shaping to be an excellent season for both Hartson, who scored 24 goals, and Berkovic, who must have made at least fifteen of them.

In the following game, another youngster, Jason Moore, made his debut for West Ham as a substitute at Southampton. Like David Terrier, he too never played again for the Hammers. Lee Hodges (five appearances as substitute), Paolo Alves (four as substitute) and Scott Mean (three as substitute) also failed to make a start that season. (see also Shaun Byrne, Chris Coyne and Gavin Holligan).

1 Ludek Miklosko, 2 Tim Breacker, 20 Andy Impey, 6 David Unsworth, 15 Rio Ferdinand, 19 Ian Pearce, 18 Frank Lampard, 14 Iain Dowie, 10 John Hartson, 29 Eyal Berkovic, 11 Steve Lomas (capt).

Scorers: John Hartson 15, Eyal Berkovic 65
MoM: Eyal Berkovic
West Ham ended the season: 8th out of 20, with 56 points.

| Number: 84 | 1997-98 | Premiership |
| 10th January 1998 | Barnsley (h) | Att: 23,714 |

WEST HAM 6 BARNSLEY 0

Despite a top-half league position for the first time in over ten years, West Ham hadn't scored six in the top division since putting eight past Newcastle in April 1986. Harry Redknapp was clearly excited by the first genuinely successful foreign signing, a player who could make goals and might stay more than a few weeks at the club. Samassi Abou, a silky skills striker from the Ivory Coast, had played in France at the top level for AS Cannes and Lyon. Abou sported wild dreadlocks, as if from a thousand-volt shock, and there was electricity in his West Ham performances. His first goal came in 1-2 League Cup quarter-final defeat by Arsenal, followed four days later by two more against Barnsley. Redknapp was also giving a decent run to Australian winger Stan Lazaridis, who played his part in this memorable victory.

Hammers had begun the season with a win at Barnsley, so now had the chance to complete their second Premiership 'double', just a fortnight after their first, over Wimbledon. Danny Wilson's Barnsley had struggled in the Premiership but were still comfortably above bottom club Crystal Palace. Hammers lay eighth, anticipating a possible European place for the first time in eighteen years.

It was a grand occasion for captain-for-the-day David Unsworth, who crossed from the left to make a headed goal for Frank Lampard on the near post. Despite scoring a home Milk Cup hat-trick against Walsall earlier in the season, this was Lampard's first home league goal, to cherish alongside his first ever goal, at Barnsley. Goal-happy John Hartson turned goal-maker for the second with a chipped ball to Abou, who fended off two Barnsley defenders to steer the ball past Watson. Cue the latest fans' creative chant – a prolonged sonorous 'Aboooooo ...' all round the ground – probably the first time a player has been booed for scoring a goal. A boo for Abou.

After half-time Abou came out with an even greater spring in his step, culminating in his putting away Hartson's one-two touch with a sublime flick of the right foot.

John Moncur was growing in confidence. He had scored stunning goals for Swindon and Tottenham before coming to Upton Park, and it was his cross from the left that set up Abou's second goal. Moncur struck the fourth after a neat one-two with Abou, hitting a crisp rasping left foot drive that beat Watson. It was the flicks that made Spurs sick – Berkovic picked out Abou with a through ball, and another touch of that right foot cleared the way for Hartson's finish and West Ham's fifth. The final goal was scored in injury-time by 'Skippy', the imaginitively nicknamed Antipodean Lazaridis, after an Abou-like flick from Hartson had put him clear. His left-foot finish almost split the net.

West Ham's winning margin had established a goal-difference of +2, which they were sadly unable to maintain, despite finishing 8th. The final count was: scored 56, conceded 57, the closest they'd come to a positive goal-difference since 1985-86. As for Abou, his three goals in two games lost their glitter when he was sent off against Spurs for remonstrating with the referee just before half-time. Trevor Sinclair's arrival soon afterwards (he netted five goals in his first six games), relegated Abou to the status of an almost great. His last achievement was to score two in the final game of the season, a 4-3 victory over Leicester, following Hartson's end-of-season four-game ban.

22 Craig Forrest, 4 Steve Potts, 17 Stan Lazaridis, 6 David Unsworth (capt), 15 Rio Ferdinand, 19 Ian Pearce, 20 Andy Impey, 18 Frank Lampard, 10 John Hartson, 29 Eyal Berkovic, 24 Samassi Abou, 16 John Moncur, 30 Paolo Alves.

Scorers:Lampard 5, Abou 31, 52, Moncur 57, Hartson 67, Lazaridis 90
MoM: Samassi Abou
West Ham ended the season: 8th out of 20, with 56 points.

Number: 85	1998-99	Premiership
9th September 1998	Wimbledon (h)	Att: 25,311

WEST HAM 3 WIMBLEDON 4

Ian Wright quit the BBC Commentary team in April 2008, claiming he wasn't having his views taken seriously – he had, as he put it, become the 'court jester'. The problem was, perhaps, that Wright was the one taking himself too seriously. Redknapp's acquisition of Neil 'Razor' Ruddock from Liverpool, another 'court jester' character, had Hammers fans wondering quite what Harry was up to. Had the training ground become a morgue? A place where there were no longer any laughs? Would the new signings bring a laugh-a-minute atmosphere back to the land of East London's finest?

What was funny was that Harry played Javier Margas, a Chilean international centre-back, alongside Neil Ruddock, with winger Stan Lazaridis playing out of position at right-back. That should have been enough to make anyone laugh, let alone those who were aware that Margas spoke no English. Goodness only knows what conversations must have passed for tactics in the first few minutes of this game.

In the event, Hammers came out of the proverbial traps like proverbs. 'Slow and steady wins the race' might have been preferable to 'he who hesitates is lost'. Hartson hit an early first goal, as the Hammers' defence remained untested through inaction. Ian Wright was at his bewildering best in the one season he was with West Ham, and his two goals inside thirteen minutes sent West Ham into a 3-0 lead within half an hour. Even the previous season's rout against Barnsley had only been 2-0 at half-time. This was Hammers' fourth game of the season and they had yet to concede a goal. Who in the crowd of partisan fans could feel it was anything other than party time?

Unlike Barnsley, Wimbledon had a few match winners in their ranks, and often took a while to warm up. Marcus Gayle pulled one back, but there was still nothing to stop fans rushing to the half-time bars to anticipate the goalfest that was certain to follow.

And follow it did. A misunderstanding between Ruddock and Margas let in Jason Euell for the Dons' second. Then a third from Gayle, after Impey had tumbled over Shaka Hislop. And then a heart-stopping fourth as Efan Ekoku headed in Euell's cross. If Hammers had blitzed down the flanks to destroy Wimbledon in the first half-hour, the homeless hatefuls had exploited a combination of complacency and naivety in the West Ham defence. It wasn't an understatement to say that in the final ten minutes Wimbledon should have broken the 35-five-year old record held by Blackburn for their 8-2 Upton Park win. As it was, Wimbledon seemed satisfied with a remarkable 4-3 win after being 0-3 down.

Hammers hosted unbeaten Liverpool three days later on the Saturday and, being Hammers, beat them 2-1 for the second season in succession. Because that's the sort of thing that West Ham do. Maybe Ian Wright finally saw the funny side after all.

12 Shaka Hislop, 8 Trevor Sinclair, 17 Stan Laziridis, 19 Ian Pearce, 30 Javier Margas, 6 Neil Ruddock, 18 Frank Lampard, 29 Eyal Berkovic, 10 John Hartson (capt), 14 Ian Wright, 16 John Moncur, 20 Andy Impey.

Scorers: Ian Wright 14, 27, John Hartson 7
MoM: Shaka Hislop
West Ham ended the season: 5th out of 20, with 57 points.

Number: 86	1999-2000	Inter Toto F2
24th August 1999	FC Metz (a)	Att: 19,599

FC METZ 1 WEST HAM 3

'We're all going on a European Tour / A European Tour / A European Tour.' So sang the Hammers' fans after this victory, though the truth was that the tour had already extended to Finland and Holland before this memorable evening in France. This was the second leg of the Inter Toto Cup final, West Ham trailing by one goal from the home game a fortnight earlier, when Frank Lampard had a rare penalty miss. He was to develop a penalty-taking neurosis later with England and Chelsea.

West Ham's 'one season wonder' brigade had featured Ian Wright the previous season, and this season it would be Costa Rican showman Paulo Wanchope, whose fifteen goals saw him miss out on the top goalscoring Hammer award by one goal, by the 'other Paulo', Paolo Di Canio.

So just how did Hammers get into Europe when finishing 5th had denied them a place? It's as unanswerable as the other question about that previous season. How come Hammers could finish 5th, their second best ever, yet their leading scorer did not make double figures?

The Inter Toto Cup, regarded by those who for one reason or another can't be bothered to enter it, is actually a back door route into Europe, provided you win your section. This usually involves six to eight games, playing teams from Latvia and Luxembourg, and a disruption of the pre-season. Hammers, however, felt so aggrieved at missing out that Harry said, 'We'll do it.' This game against Metz was their sixth, and they required at least two away goals to avoid a penalty shoot-out. Somehow they scored them before half-time, great finishes from Sinclair, after Di Canio set him up, and Lampard, atoning for his first-leg penalty miss with a fine angled shot.

The travelling fans were enjoying something they'd been sick of hearing their fathers boast about for twenty years, a European Tour. If Hammers could hold their nerve, they'd be in the draw for the first round proper of the UEFA Cup. As it was, Jestrovic pulled Metz level in the tie, and it took a goal from man-of-the-match Wanchope ten minutes later to give Hammers that all-important aggregate lead and, as it turned out, their first trophy in some time.

The post-match presentation may have been a farce, but the fans did not care – this was their moment, an away victory in Europe to cherish, and proof that Redknapp had got the Academy of Football back on the map after many years in the wilderness. It was taking him squads of 29 as opposed to the squad of eighteen that finished third in the old First Division in 1985-86, but things were different in the moneyland of the Premiership.

And what about that squad? Stuart Pearce had arrived, crocking his teammate namesake Ian on his debut, so there wouldn't be any more scrapping for the team shirt. As luck wouldn't have it, Pearce then broke his own leg in his fifth match, against Watford's Micah Hyde, and was out for the season. Michael Carrick made the grade through to the first team ahead of Joe Cole, and Redknapp made his mandatory foreign defender purchases, Croatian Igor Stimac and, from Cameroon, Marc-Vivien Foe. The most remarkable arrival of all, however, was Redknapp's master-stroke, on a par with John Lyall's discovery of Frank McAvennie, the signing of 'bad boy', sin-binned Paolo Di Canio for just £1.5 million.

1 Shaka Hislop, 11 Steve Lomas (capt), 15 Rio Ferdinand, 4 Steve Potts, 8 Trevor Sinclair, 18 Frank Lampard, 13 Marc-Vivien Foe, 16 John Moncur, 7 Marc Keller, 10 Paolo Di Canio, 12 Paulo Wanchope, 26) Joe Cole.

Scorers: Sinclair 23, Lampard 43, Wanchope 78
MoM: Paulo Wanchope
West Ham ended the season: 9th out of 20, with 55 points.

Number: 87	1999-2000	Premier ship
3rd October 1999	Arsenal (h)	Att: 26,009

WEST HAM 2 ARSENAL 1

The last occasion West Ham had beaten Arsenal in the league had been the Liam Brady showcase back in April 1987 (No 64). It was another import who stole the show and finally cemented his place in the hearts of all West Ham fans, one Paolo Di Canio.

Di Canio had finished the previous season with some maverick per-formances, but had started 1999-2000 with three goals in the first seven league games, two of them winners, and had the crowd chanting his name to the tune of *La Donna e Mobile* . There was a swagger and an arrogance in Di Canio's demeanour that was half self-mocking and half anything-but. Defenders didn't know how to contain him, and never more so than against Arsenal now. The England defence of Adams and Keown, all righteous self-help and neanderthalism, were made to look as ridiculous in their play as they did in their appearance.

The BBC picked their best commentator, the regal Barry Davies, rather than the stat-laden John Motson, and it was an inspired choice. Davies sat with his less-than-objective (on this occasion) summariser, Trevor Brooking, extolling the genius of the Ljungbergs, the Vieiras, the Bergkamps and the great Henry. Halfway through Davies' worshipful dia-tribe, Paolo Di Canio began a run from inside his own half, beating three Arsenal players, before the ball broke to Trevor Sinclair, who dragged it back for Di Canio to force over the line. For a moment everyone was convinced the ball had gone out, or that Di Canio was offside, or that the assistant referee would disallow it anyway just for the hell of it ... but the goal stood. West Ham went in at half-time a goal up against 'the' Arsenal. It seemed hard to believe, Davies certainly didn't believe it, but as the game wore on, all that happened was that Henry, Ljungberg and Bergkamp were marked out of the game, and Suker, who wasn't, missed chance after chance. Then the goal.

It began as classic route one. A kick from Hislop hit high towards the edge of the Arsenal penalty area, Hammers pushing up. Adams, towering in the air behind Wanchope, was only able to help the ball backwards. Di Canio, all legs and sway, swivelled, flicked the ball over Keown's head, and lifted the ball delicately over the pony-tailed David Seaman, who'd been caught off his line enough times never to play for his country again. This was Seaman, whose body-check professional foul on Trevor Morley all those years ago saw him sent off, the same week he had conceded an eight second goal against San Marino.

This time Di Canio was too good to be denied. It was certainly one of the greatest individual moments ever seen at Upton Park. Up there with Hurst's six, Banks' save, 'Pop' Robson's hat-trick, Keith Robson's Euro-Belter, Kenny Brown's thump against United, Bonds' Chelsea hat-trick, Alan Taylor's route one effort, Cottee's debut header v Spurs, Alvin's hat-trick past three different keepers ... certainly up there with all of those. And Barry Davies? 'Utterly superb. And so against the run of play it's not true.' He shouldn't have said that with Trevor in the commentary box, but it didn't matter. The pictures told the story. Genius will not be denied.

And against Arsenal. It would have been brilliant against anyone. But Arsenal! If he had been melting West Ham hearts before this, he had melted them for ever now.

The second piece of genius, and final act of revenge for Willie Young's foul on Paul Allen in the 1980 FA Cup final, that denied my dad nearly £200 for the bet he'd had on a 2-0 finish, was carried out by Neil Ruddock. What he lacked in determination and international experience over Adams and Keown, he made up for in guile. Ruddock had spent most of the match winding up Henry and Viera in the Sid James style of 'Carry on Henry'. Despite the immaturity of Ruddock's niggling jibes, Patrick Vieira finally cracked. He upended the irritant Di Canio for a second yellow, and dismissal. Incredibly, having left the field, the Frenchman had a second 'snapping' and returned to spit at his tormentor Ruddock, who laughed disparagingly to accentuate the personal torment. Referee Mike Reed had been on booking patrol throughout the game, and waved

Vieira back off the field, unsympathetic at his desire to share bodily fluids with his marker.

Suker pulled one back for Arsenal, and Foe was dismissed for a second red after a tackle from behind on Bergkamp, but it stayed 2-1.

1 Shaka Hislop, 11 Steve Lomas (capt), 5 Igor Stimac, 13 Marc-Vivien Foe, 4 Steve Potts, 6 Neil Ruddock, 10 Paolo Di Canio, 18 Frank Lampard, 16 John Moncur, 12 Paulo Wanchope, 8 Trevor Sinclair, 30 Javier Margas, 9 Paul Kitson.

Scorer: Paolo Di Canio 29, 72
MoM: Paolo Di Canio
West Ham ended the season: 9th out of 20, with 55 points.

Number: 88	1999-2000	Premiership
12th February 2000	Bradford City (h)	Att: 25,417

WEST HAM 5 BRADFORD CITY 4

This match had just about everything. Nine goals, broken legs, rows over penalty-taking, a major wobbly from Di Canio, a black goalscorer with red hair, and an eighteen-year-old debutant goalkeeper conceding four goals and still ending up on the winning side!

Less than three minutes had passed when Hislop broke his leg in a challenge with Dean Saunders. Hammers had given Neil Finn a debut on New Year's Day 1996, after Ludek Miklosko's suspension, the youngest ever Premiership keeper at 17 years and 3 days. Now Stephen Bywater was to follow – just 18 years and 250 days old. What must he have been thinking? And how might the game have gone had he not been between the sticks that afternoon?

What was also strange was that one third of the game passed goalless until Dean Windass headed Bradford ahead from an inswinging corner. Five minutes later Gary Charles, in his second of only two West Ham starts – the first of which had yielded a late own-goal winner seven days earlier for Southampton – started the move that led to Hammers' equaliser. Steve Lomas turned quickly and was floored, but before referee Neal Barry could blow for a penalty, Trevor Sinclair gathered the loose ball, spun, and hit his seventh goal of the season. Bizarrely for Charles, despite his key role in the match, he was never picked to start another game for the Hammers.

Just before half-time, John Moncur hit another of his wonder goals, collecting Di Canio's swiftly taken free-kick before rifling an unstoppable shot into the far corner of the net. The replay shows he had lost his balance in the act of striking the ball, which contributed to its away trajectory. In his celebration, Moncur removed his shirt, revealing not the regulation white vest, but a shocking navy t-shirt that might have been plundered from a local pound shop.

The extended injury-time for Hislop's leg break allowed Bradford time to head up the other end of the pitch, where momentary hero Moncur felled Saunders to force Bywater into facing a penalty. There were to be no heroics for the debutant keeper, despite lip-reading revelations of him mouthing, 'Save the f****** ball, save the f****** ball' as Beagrie stepped up to put it past him. Despite their dreadful away record, Paul Jewell's men went in at the break on level terms.

It took City just six second-half minutes to coast into a 4-2 lead. Both goals were scored by the red-clown-haired Jamie Lawrence, but the manner of their arrival would have infuriated Redknapp. Hovering on the edge of the box, Bradford's Halle hit a speculative shot at Bywater, which he fielded before dropping it into the path of Lawrence, who bundled it over the line.

Four minutes later Lawrence found himself in almost the exact spot from where Moncur had scored earlier. Lawrence's shot had power, height and dip, that caught Bywater marginally off his line, unable to keep it out. Three minutes later Dean Saunders beat Bywater again, for a potential fifth, but his shot came back off the post.

Poor Bywater had conceded four goals in 22 minutes, setting his teammates an improbable mountain to climb in the half-hour remaining. It seemed to be a day of reckoning for the Hammers when Di Canio was unceremoniously upended for a second time. This time his histrionic protestations were again ignored by referee Neil Barry.

Upton Park has had a few Twilight Zone moments over the years, but something was about to happen that was unprecedented in the history of the club. Hardly surprising that Paolo Di Canio was the focal point. Referee Barry was a paid-up member of the 'No Penalties For Di Canio' union, presumably formed after the Italian's shove on Paul Alcock two years previously. After yet another fruitless appeal, the Italian stormed over to the dugout while the game flowed around him and demanded that Redknapp take him off, gesturing wildly at the man in black as the cause of his grief. After a few phrases of Anglo-Saxon encouragement from Redknapp, Di Canio returned to the action, accompanied by the oncoming substitute for Gary Charles, Paul Kitson.

Were Bradford City undone by this unique moment of unthinkable petulance? Was this actually part of a bigger plan from the creative genius that irrational grudges should never be part of a referee's armoury? The assembled 25,417 witnessed something no crowd had ever seen before or since. The first and only Public Premier League Sulk. Check those Opta Stats in your club programme – this is the only sulk that's ever been recorded in the Premiership.

In West Ham's very next attack, Kitson lost his footing in the box after close marking from O'Brien. The ref pointed to the spot. And who is the penalty taker for the Hammers? Since missing against Aston Villa the previous month, Di Canio had vowed never to take another. Armed with this revelation, Frank Lampard grabbed the ball and was already at the penalty spot. Another Twilight Zone moment. The two players, Lampard and Di Canio, jabbing fingers at each other over who should take it. With a third goal, Hammers would be back in the game, but if the chance was missed, it was unlikely they could recover. Di Canio's seniority won out, and thankfully he tucked the penalty away.

Joe Cole, barely eighteen, was Bywater's junior by five months, but had enjoyed a run in the first team, having made his debut a year previously, even before Di Canio's arrival. Now Cole burst through on the right and hit an improbable equaliser from a tight angle. With two goals in five minutes, Hammers now had twenty minutes to find a winner. Bradford City heads were down, but it took a further quarter of an hour before Frank Lampard found space and time to volley home.

At the final whistle the crowd applauded both teams off. Only one West Ham player looked crestfallen. Goalkeeper Stephen Bywater, inconsolable, despite the amazing victory. He would not don a first-team shirt again for another year, also against Bradford City, but this time at Valley Parade in a 2-1 victory. He would wait even longer for appearance number three – three years – against Sheffield United in the First Division, in a 3-3 draw in which he saved a penalty.

As for Di Canio, the following month he manufactured an event just as astonishing. From helping create the Premiership's greatest ever game, he managed a goal against Wimbledon that people still refer to as the greatest ever scored in the Premiership. He finished the season top scorer with seventeen goals, a worthy winner of Hammer of the Year.

1 Shaka Hislop, 15 Rio Ferdinand, 5 Igor Stimac, 20 Scott Minto, 2 Gary Charles, 11 Steve Lomas (capt), 18 Frank Lampard, 16 John Moncur, 26 Joe Cole, 10 Paolo Di Canio, 8 Trevor Sinclair, 32 Steve Bywater, 9 Paul Kitson.

Scorers: Sinclair 35, Moncur 43, Cole 70, Di Canio 65p, Lampard 83
MoM: Paolo Di Canio
West Ham ended the season: 9th out of 20, with 55 points.

Number: 89	2000-01	Premiership
26th December 2000	Charlton Athletic (h)	Att: 26,046

WEST HAM 5 CHARLTON 0

This was the Boxing Day when 26,000 Hammers' fans chose to consume football instead of turkey curry – though there was certainly something spicy about this affair, with Hammers the vindaloo to Charlton's korma.

A few weeks after the Bradford City fiesta, Harry Redknapp signed the tall, wily French striker Frederic 'Fredi' Kanoute, who began scoring goals with a finesse that had fans drooling. With Michael Carrick coming through the ranks, Redknapp had kept creativity at the forefront of West Ham's play, even though Rio Ferdinand had earlier departed for Leeds after starring in the Hammers' side that beat them (1-0) at Elland Road for the first time since 1978. Other than Liverpool, Leeds were perhaps the pick of the bogey sides away from Upton Park.

Boxing Day games traditionally offered plenty of goals. The 2-8 home defeat by Blackburn in 1963, a 4-1 victory at Blackpool in 1966, 4-2 v Leicester in 1967, a 4-2 win at Chelsea in 1973, 4-0 over Derby in 2001 and 3-2 against Nottingham Forest in 2004, all evidence of Christmas cheer, usually from the opposition's defence.

Richard Rufus, not for the first time in his career, deflected a shot from Di Canio to put the Hammers ahead. Then came a stunning move. Di Canio, then Kanoute, then Sinclair and finally Kanoute, off the hapless last defender, exchanged flicks and passes as if on a training ground. This one was finished by Kanoute, angling his body like a pirouetting figure skater as he flicked the ball past Kiely. If only he didn't wear those silly woollen gloves.

Next up in the Christmas talent show was Di Canio, who dragged the Charlton defence this way and that on the left before pulling over a cross that Lampard had only to blow on to help it over the line.

The second half brought only two more goals, the first a breathtaking 25-yard volley from Trevor Sinclair. The last word on the game was provided after a through ball from Carrick that the long legs of Kanoute controlled before he scored arrogantly. Victory carried the Hammers to 8th as they saw in the New Year.

1 Shaka Hislop, 11 Steve Lomas (capt), 17 Nigel Winterburn, 8 Trevor
Sinclair, 15 Rigobert Song, 3 Stuart Pearce, 18 Frank Lampard, 29 Titi
Camara, 14 Fredi Kanoute, 10 Paolo Di Canio, 21 Michael Carrick, 26 Joe
Cole, 16 John Moncur, 28 Hannu Tihinen.

Scorers: Rufus 13 (og), Kanoute 18, 84, Lampard 45, Sinclair 71
MoM: Trevor Sinclair
West Ham ended the season: 15th out of 20, with 42 points.

| Number: 90 | 2000-01 | FA Cup R4 |
| 28th January 2001 | Manchester United (a) | Att: 67,029 |

MANCHESTER UNITED 0 WEST HAM 1

Playing in front of three times as many spectators as could be squeezed
into Upton Park, West Ham produced a wonder display to oust the
League Champions from the FA Cup on their own ground. What was
perhaps more surprising was that they had fallen 1-3 in the league earlier
in the month to a United side that stretched their Premiership lead to
eleven points. The year before West Ham had been walloped 1-7.

ITV covered this game live, and only one side was expected to win.
United were at full strength, and Beckham, Keane, Gary Neville, Giggs
and Sheringham were all on top form.

One of Hammers' new loan signings was Icelandic international
Hannu Tihinen, a diminutive defensive midfielder with a sharp football
brain. Now starting his third game, he marshalled the defence with
Schemmel, alongside the experienced Dailly, Winterburn and Stuart
Pearce. Hislop, after receiving an early knock, required more cover than
usual, but still had it in him to make a superb save late in the first half
from a dipping Beckham free-kick, which curled over the West Ham
defensive wall.

The creative engine of Cole, Carrick and Lampard kept Kanoute and
Di Canio busy trying to find a way through the home defence. Though
United created plenty of opportunities early on, the Hammers' defence
held firm, and Cole and Carrick kept maverick keeper Fabien Barthez
busy with shots from distance.

As the game progressed, Hammers took the measure of their opponents on a pitch horribly rutted by the Rugby League World Cup final a
few days' earlier. Then came the moment all West Ham fans' craved.
Kanoute trapped the ball and, with the United back four raising their

arms, Kanoute toe-poked the ball past Gary Neville to Di Canio, running across the United defence.

Everyone in the ground but Di Canio was sure his run had been timed badly, and that the nonchalant raised arms of the United defence for an offside flag were correct. They were not. As Di Canio drew Barthez from his goal, the French keeper also raised his arm. But Di Canio was not to be fooled. The kidder could not kid The Kidder. Di Canio swept the ball into the unguarded net.

Any goal against United at this late stage would have been welcomed with a hurricane cheer from the 9,000 travelling Hammers' fans, but these celebrations seemed to go on for ever. Keane was complaining, Beckham was complaining, Neville was complaining, long after three replays of the goal from three different angles had proved to anyone watching them that the referee's assistant was correct.

'It's West Ham United who take the lead!' yelled Clive Tyldsley. 'It's Par-loh Di Carny-oh!' No one had ever spoken the Italian maestro's name with such peculiar pronunciation, but it remains a section of commentary cemented into the frontal lobes of all Hammers' fans. Having proved himself to be the clown of the afternoon, it was fitting that Barthez was in possession of the ball in the West Ham half, attempting to redeem his earlier madness by scoring an unlikely goal, when the final whistle went. He lashed the ball into the crowd with more venom than any of his clearances during the game.

With another victory at Sunderland in the fifth round, it should have been West Ham's FA Cup year, twenty years on, but in the rain and mud they stumbled at home to Tottenham and went down 2-3, exiting the Cup along with Spurs' boss George Graham who left his position the following week to become a football pundit.

Harry Redknapp followed Graham two months later after falling out with the West Ham board over cash for new players, the same cash that had not been made available to buy Hannu Tihinen when he came up for sale.

1 Shaka Hislop, 30 Sebastien Schemmel, 17 Nigel Winterburn, 28 Hannu Tihinen, 7 Christian Dailly, 3 Stuart Pearce (capt), 18 Frank Lampard, 26 Joe Cole, 21 Michael Carrick, 10 Paolo Di Canio, 14 Fredi Kanoute, 19 Ian Pearce, 29 Ragnvald Soma.

Scorer: Paolo Di Canio 76
MoM: Joe Cole
West Ham ended the season: 15th out of 20, with 42 points.

Number: 91   2001-02   Premiership
19th November 2001   Charlton Athletic (a)   Att: 23,198

CHARLTON 4 WEST HAM 4

Jermain Defoe made his West Ham league debut against Middlesbrough in the last game of 2000-01, Glenn Roeder's first as manager. No one was more surprised to be put in charge at West Ham than Roeder himself. He had spent most of the season looking after youth team players like Defoe, shielding them from the limelight that he now stepped into so unexpectedly. The game at Charlton was the first time Defoe had faced his former club since his acrimonious departure from the Valley, and he quickly learned what it was like to be booed every time he went near the ball. Thankfully, he started on West Ham's bench, still awaiting an automatic place, despite his goalscoring prowess at every level.

This game, because of injury to Fredi Kanoute, tested Roeder's selection skills. Defoe wasn't deemed ready to start, so Roeder turned to his reserve striker Paul Kitson, who had been in the West Ham wilderness for two years since being dropped by Redknapp shortly after the 5-4 victory over Bradford City. It had been a long time away from first-team action for Kitson, but he had trained hard and taken in two short loan periods (six games) at Charlton and Crystal Palace, during which he scored four goals. This was the last season of his West Ham contract so, nearly 31, this was clearly a final throw of the career dice.

On this cold November night, Kitson was like a dead man walking, his skinny shape appearing at the near and far posts to connect with crosses from Sinclair and Di Canio. He had always been a six-yard box man, but had also shown pace and awareness, clear from the seventeen goals he had scored in his 46 appearances for the club. On this night he was everywhere, pouncing on mistakes from defenders, and there were plenty of those in Curbishley's wayward Charlton. Sadly for Roeder, missing the experience of Winterburn and adopting a defensive formation that looked naïve, goals were leaking at the other end, too.

Kitson's quick opener was wiped out by Jason Euell, and then Euell hit a second. Kitson equalised within a minute, but Jonatan Johansson restored Charlton's lead early in the second half. Incredibly Kitson completed his return-from-the-dead hat-trick to spare the defenders' blushes. With each of his goals, Kitson offered a low-key celebration worthy of a 1950s footballer, something he often seemed to be. It was as if he knew his return was only temporary and – like Hamlet's father, returned from the dead to speak – Kitson resurfaced to remind West Ham fans of how his and John Hartson's goals saved them from certain relegation in the 1996-97 season.

Never one to court nostalgia, Roeder substituted Kitson before the end, bringing on Defoe to the derision of angry Charlton fans. Charlton – the family club – whose supporters are just like any other's, if the truth be known. Defoe, who would endure a similar response from the West Ham crowd later when he joined Tottenham, shrugged off the insults to score a fine goal six minutes from the end to restore the Hammers' lead. They might even have won the game but for an injury-time overhead kick from Johansson that made it 4-4.

Kitson was given just two more league starts that season, but scored goals for Brighton, Rushden & Diamonds and Aldershot in later years. Defoe submitted his transfer request to Roeder an hour or so after the club were relegated the following season, partly as a result of his own inability to put away the many chances provided for him.

This was also Shaka Hislop's last game under Roeder, now that David James was finally fit after being injured before he could make his debut. James would stay two more years, but his goals-conceded record at West Ham was always inferior to Hislop's, who returned under Alan Pardew.

17 Shaka Hislop, 30 Sebastien Schemmel, 20 Scott Minto, 6 Hayden Foxe, 2 Thomas Repka, 7 Christian Dailly, 8 Trevor Sinclair, 4 Don Hutchison, 12 Paul Kitson, 10 Paolo Di Canio, 21 Michael Carrick, 26 Joe Cole, 25 Jermain Defoe, 11 Steve Lomas (capt).

Scorers: Paul Kitson 3, 30, 64, Jermain Defoe 84
MoM: Paul Kitson
West Ham ended the season: 7th out of 20, with 53 points.

Number: 92	2002-03	Premiership
28th September 2002	Chelsea (a)	Att: 38,929

CHELSEA 2 WEST HAM 3

Glenn Roeder will almost certainly be remembered at West Ham not for guiding his players to 7th in his first season, but for relegating a team blessed with eighteen full internationals (and the seventh best supported club in the Premiership). Granted it was the players who lost the matches, but Roeder's intransigence with his stars and his unpredictable style of management clearly contributed to the club's problems.

Roeder's main problem was with Di Canio. Sulky, moody, two-paced ... and Di Canio wasn't much better. The Italian, given a free rein by Redknapp in his glory years, was soon made to understand that Roeder's West Ham was an egalitarian outfit, without room for big heads and egos. The kids who had grown up there with Roeder liked this – the Defoes, Johnsons, Coles and Carricks. The older professionals, including Di Canio, Winterburn and Breen, might have learned something from them. When Roeder named Joe Cole captain in November, it couldn't have pleased those at the club who had felt the honour ought to have been theirs.

By their seventh game, Hammers had mustered just two points out of a possible eighteen, their worst ever start in any league. Not a great time to face Claudio Ranieri's Chelsea, who had finished just one place above them the previous season, yet would finish this one in fourth place. A hostile Stamford Bridge saw Hasselbainck put Chelsea ahead from the spot after twenty minutes, but the rout did not materialise. Instead, despite Kanoute hobbling off early on from an injury that would sideline him for most of the season, they came back into the game, inspired by Cole, Carrick and Sinclair's mastery of midfield, and Di Canio's trickery up front. Just before half-time Defoe, who after the next match would not miss another all season, tucked away an equaliser.

Di Canio might not have seen eye to eye with Roeder (it was said they weren't on speaking terms at the training ground) but he never lost his affection for the reciprocal West Ham crowd. Shortly after half-time, receiving the ball 40 yards out, he hit a stupendous volley beyond countryman Cudicini into the far corner of the net. From the noise, it seemed he had scored at Upton Park. Maybe the players could hear the roars from the 5,000 ticketless fans who had made the journey that day to Upton Park to watch a live beamback of the game on the big screens.

It was a good day for Italian geniuses; Gianfranco Zola, later to manage West Ham, put away an equalising free-kick and it looked as though Hammers would have to settle for a point. Rising to the occasion as only he could, Di Canio had other ideas. Strolling through the Chelsea defence, he pulled wide on the left-hand side, too wide it seemed, until he hit a controlled near-post shot that caught out Cudicini. Again the emotional celebrations. Some who were at the game said that the Chelsea fans were cheering, too. That's what fans used to do at football games, or so my father told me. They would cheer even when a player from the opposition scored a superb goal. This is entertainment, after all, and if you've paid money to watch someone entertain, and they entertain you, shouldn't you applaud?

It could have been the Italian connection, but after the game Claudio Ranieri was not sparing in his praise of Di Canio, who he declared had been the difference between the two sides. Di Canio had made his statement on the pitch, and did not make himself available for interview, but Roeder, often impossibly shy and awkward in front of the cameras, went out to say his piece and praise Di Canio's efforts. It was a good time for plaudits, as Hammers had just won their first game of the season. The home hoodoo continued, but West Ham won two of their next three matches and climbed to fourteenth. It would, sadly, be another fifteen games until their next win, only their fourth all season and their first at home for eight months.

1 David James, 30 Sebastien Schemmel, 20 Scott Minto, 11 Steve Lomas (capt), 2 Tomas Repka, 15 Gary Breen, 8 Trevor Sinclair, 26 Joe Cole, 14 Fredi Kanoute, 10 Paolo Di Canio, 6 Michael Carrick, 9 Jermain Defoe.

Scorers: Jermain Defoe 40, Paolo Di Canio 48, 84
MoM: Paolo Di Canio
West Ham ended the season: 18/20 with 42 points (relegated).

Number: 93	2002-03	Premiership
3rd May 2003	Chelsea (h)	Att: 35,042

WEST HAM 1 CHELSEA 0

West Ham fans had waited 36 years, in vain it always seemed, to see any real emotion flash across the face of Trevor Brooking at Upton Park. Fate would take a giant hand in April 2003 to make that rare moment happen. All who saw the gleam in his eyes as Brooking punched the air to celebrate Paolo Di Canio's 71st-minute goal against Chelsea, the last he would ever score at Upton Park, knew that they were momentarily in the presence of angels.

The only similarity between this game and the earlier one that season against Chelsea, would prove to be the genius of Di Canio. Was he the most skilful player ever to don a West Ham shirt? The arguments will continue, but for Hammers' fans mourning the fact that he only started sixteen of the 38 Premier League games that season, there is little doubt that Di Canio's too-frequent absences from the side was the source of the lack of goals and the drop in spirit that the club suffered over the course of this awful, miserable season.

Moments after the home win over Middlesbrough a fortnight earlier, Roeder had suffered a minor stroke, effectively unable to take any further part in the club's season. With only three games to go and a precariously slim chance of avoiding relegation, Trevor Brooking volunteered to play caretaker manager for the final fortnight.

This was Di Canio's 49th West Ham goal (he would reach his half-century the following Sunday at Birmingham), but it was memorable for many more reasons than that.

What could perhaps be his final Upton Park appearance, though his goal raised hopes it might not be, was as a substitute for the last half-hour in place of the spent Les Ferdinand. The fantastic reception he got from fans was even more remarkable, seeing as for most of the match they had shouted themselves hoarse at Chelsea's, on the day rather ineffectual, Francis Lampard.

Up to Di Canio's arrival there had been little to report in the way of goalmouth action but with news of Bolton drawing against Southampton Trevor Sinclair, out on the right, blasted a hopeful shot-come-cross. Di Canio connected with the ball in the six yard box to steer it home— an unusually, for him, orthodox striker's goal.

Eyes turned from Di Canio's emotional celebrations with teammates (his last appearance had been back in February at West Brom) back to the dugout and to Trevor Brooking, who had already stage-crafted a victory at Manchester City the previous weekend. The animated punch in the air and face that looked as though it had been inflated by an industrial wind machine caught the imagination even more than Di Canio's antics. These were two men who both loved the broken club that they were trying to keep in the Premier League.

Even if their efforts would finally prove to be in vain, this was their club and their hope against hope, the shared industry of a moment, the blurred emotion colouring in and filling every West Ham soul.

1 David James, 23 Glen Johnson, 24 Rufus Brevett, 11 Steve Lomas (capt), 2 Tomas Repka, 7 Christian Dailly, 8 Trevor Sinclair, 9 Jermain Defoe, 22 Les Ferdinand, 14 Fredi Kanoute, 26 Joe Cole, 10 Paolo Di Canio.

Scorer: Paolo Di Canio 71
MoM: Paolo Di Canio
West Ham ended the season: 18th out of 20, with 42 points (relegated).

Number: 94   2003-04   Play-Off SF 2L
12th May 2004   Ipswich Town (h)   Att: 34,002

WEST HAM 2 IPSWICH 0

Alan Pardew had taken over from Roeder and Trevor Brooking, the care-taker with the taupe shoes.

The second leg of the second play-off semi-final in the Nationwide Division One was a midweek affair under floodlights. As the clock ticked away before the game, the roar began to rise. And it was a roar. Upton Park had not sounded like that for years. Unbelievable atmosphere.

Something magical was happening. That was what this miserable, forgettable season had been about. Getting to the end of it and knowing you wouldn't have to go through it all again. The fans had eventually been won over by Alan Pardew, a man whose public personality, measured against that of Glenn Roeder, had proved inspiring.

In the other play-off semi the previous night, ex-Hammer Michael Hughes had hit the winning penalty for Crystal Palace at Sunderland in an extra time shoot-out. Likewise, West Ham could not disappoint.

All the pessimism evaporated into the East End night sky. The fans felt instantly, with a strange certainty, that they were headed for Cardiff in a couple of weeks. The West Ham side for that great night featured a return for Rufus Brevett after his injury against Sheffield United back in August. Alan Pardew kept faith with his three strikers, Harewood, Zamora and Connolly; with the whole eleven, in fact, who returned from the first leg trailing by one goal.

'Thank you for your great support this season from all the players and staff at West Ham United,' Jeremy Nicholas said over the PA. There were 5,000 fewer spectators inside than on that memorable night against Eintracht Frankfurt in 1976, but this was an all-seater stadium, a place with no reputation for atmosphere, certainly nothing like the electricity in the ground that night.

Ipswich themselves had brought nearly 5,500 fans, all making themselves heard with equal enthusiasm, all playing their part in creating a wonderful, memorable night of passionate football.

Although Ipswich won the toss and opted to kick-off, the Hammers gained possession after twenty seconds and Connolly sent Zamora away down the right. His acceleration and determination set the tone for the game. Although West Ham didn't get the early breaks, they were unhurried and professional in their approach. Now the occasion required it, they were about to produce their best football of the season.

Repka was a tower at the back, tackling with precision, letting no one behind him or beyond the back four. Christian Dailly looked unsurpassable, and Bywater commanded his area. How different from the boy he had been in that Bradford City farce. Andy Melville had seen promotion with both Fulham and Sunderland, so his experience and calmness was no surprise. As for Mullins, he knew that if West Ham won this game, he would be face to face with his Palace ex-colleagues at the Millennium Stadium in twelve days' time.

Michael Carrick was everywhere, hitting two-yard passes with the same precision as his 40-yarders to Harewood and Zamora. Carrick linked well with Steve Lomas, their midfield partnership resuscitated after the Irishman's ten-month layoff. On the left was the Hammer of the Year, Etherington, subdued in the first half, but he would compensate.

Kelvin Davis was forced into a one-handed save from Zamora's header, and then turned away a 30-yard dipper from Dailly, but the first half stayed goalless.

Kuqi was on for Ipswich at the change-round and manager Joe Royle correctly anticipated a tougher second half. Pardew made no changes. Dailly met a cross with his head, but a deflection took the ball wide for a corner. It was a short one from Carrick to Etherington, who suddenly accelerated inside before unleashing an unbelievable strike. Five minutes later, Pardew brought on Deane for Zamora. No petulance from Zamora tonight. The crowd sang, 'Deano, Deano, Deano …'

Deane won everything in the air. When the ball fell at Dailly's feet, he took a knock in the act of poking it goalwards. The ball seemed to take a lifetime before nestling in the goal, while Dailly collapsed in one of sport's 'smallest area, greatest pain' moments.

The celebrations began. Reo-Coker came on for Connolly to steady the ship and West Ham reshaped to 4-4-2. In the final minute Ian Westlake hit a swerver that beat Bywater but rebounded off the woodwork. Seconds later it was all over. The Ipswich fans sang in defeat, as both teams stayed out, ecstatic and bemused, for a further ten minutes.

Alan Pardew and his players re-emerged after ten more minutes. 'There'll be no lap of honour,' he shouted above the noise. 'Because we haven't won anything yet!' Yet West Ham had at last made Upton Park a place opponents seemed to dread. That earlier vulnerability was ironically born with a Carling Cup home defeat by Second Division Oldham Athletic, back in October 2002. Ironic, because Oldham were then managed by the man whose team West Ham would now have to face on Saturday, 29th May 2004 for a place in the Premiership, former Hammer Iain Dowie.

32 Stephen Bywater, 2 Tomas Repka, 22 Andy Melville, 7 Christian Dailly (capt), 17 Hayden Mullins, 10 Marlon Harewood, 6 Michael Carrick, 11 Steve Lomas, 12 Matthew Etherington, 8 David Connolly, 25 Bobby Zamora, 29 Brian Deane, 20 Nigel Reo-Coker.

Scorers: Matthew Etherington 50, Christian Dailly 71
MoM: Christian Dailly
West Ham ended the season: 4th out of 24, with 74 points
(lost to Crystal Palace in play-off final).

| Number: 95 | 2004-05 | Play-Off SF 2L |
| 18th May 2005 | Ipswich Town (a) | Att: 30,010 |

IPSWICH 0 WEST HAM 2

Should it have been the final? Not really; Hammers sensed they would win that now, after they had won at Joe Royle's Ipswich, who had only missed out on automatic promotion by two points after topping the league for the previous nine months.

So Hammers faced yet another play-off semi-final tussle, but because the Tractor Boys had enjoyed the better of this season and finished third to West Ham's sixth, they would play the second leg at home, having secured a vital away goal at Upton Park four days earlier. This in spite of being two goals down after thirteen minutes.

Six play-off attempts for Ipswich beforehand, and only one promotion. They bore the stigma of chokers, but they would be favourites on the night.

On the hour, however, Zamora scored with a tap-in. Hammers had seized the moment and were playing with confidence, doubling their lead eleven minutes later. Harewood played the ball out of defence and began one of his mesmerising runs, accelerating down the right. Such runs often degenerated into what some fans derided as 'headless chicken syndrome', when the ball would be run out for a goal-kick. But now, not only did Harewood keep the ball at his feet, his cross was inch-perfect, aimed at Zamora on the edge of the penalty area. Zamora met the ball delicately with his right boot and volleyed into the opposite corner of the net past Ipswich keeper Davis. 2-0. The Tractor Boys were not going to come back from that.

Hammers had finished this season sixth with 73 points, three ahead of nearest rivals Reading. The previous season they had been two places higher with 74, only to lose the play-off final against Crystal Palace. This season they would face Preston, but the fans weren't worried, because they knew after that night's win that they had done the hard bit.

23 Jimmie Walker, 2 Tomas Repka, 15 Anton Ferdinand, 22 Elliott Ward, 34 Chris Powell, 17 Hayden Mullins, 6 Carl Fletcher, 20 Nigel Reo-Coker (capt), 12 Matthew Etherington, 10 Marlon Harewood, 25 Bobby Zamora, 7 Christian Dailly, 26 Shaun Newton, 24 Mark Noble.

Scorer: Bobby Zamora 61, 72
MoM: Bobby Zamora
West Ham ended the season: 6th out of 24, with 73 points
(promoted after beating Preston in the play-off final).

Number: 96	2005-06	Premiership
1st February 2006	Arsenal (a)	Att: 38,216

ARSENAL 2 WEST HAM 3

International footballers, especially English internationals, are often blessed with the status of gods when they play abroad. This was the case with Sol Campbell, the only English player to be included in the World Cup Best XI from the 2002 tournament. At home, however, such players are open to ridicule and merriment at their expense by fans of other clubs. Campbell had enjoyed a pretty good record over the years against the Hammers, but all that changed on this February evening at Highbury, the last time the Hammers would play Arsenal before their move to the Emirates Stadium.

Arsenal had enjoyed much of the play until Campbell's miskicked clearance fell into the path of Nigel Reo-Coker, who finished well and put West Ham in front. Campbell's second error was even better, Zamora shrugging him off with ease before firing past Lehmann. Hammers' Clive Clarke was making one of only two career appearances that evening – a game he would never forget. Thierry Henry, who had been inconspicuous for most of the game, put Arsenal back in contention before half-time, deflecting a Robert Pires shot past Shaka Hislop to become the highest scorer in Arsenal's history.

Mysteriously, Sol Campbell not only left the pitch at half-time, but left the ground too, heading goodness knows where, as he reflected on his contribution to West Ham's lead. Even the rarely ruffled Arsene Wenger began making inappropriately high-pitched squeaks once he realised his top international centre-back had temporarily 'lost it'.

Late in the second half Matthew Etherington sealed victory with a third goal that even Pires' later second for Arsenal would not equal. The nightmare for Arsenal was complete. Knocked out of the Cup by Bolton and now beaten at home by the Hammers, and with their England centre-back gone AWOL.

Victories against Arsenal in recent years have been rare, but the timing and substance of this win was especially pleasing. Hammers would be the last team to win at Highbury in a fixture between the two clubs, so who was to say that they wouldn't repeat the offence the following season at the all-new Emirates Stadium?

34 Shaka Hislop, 30 Clive Clarke, 5 Anton Ferdinand, 4 Danny Gabbidon, 3 Paul Konchesky, 15 Yossi Benayoun, 17 Hayden Mullins, 20 Nigel Reo-Coker (capt), 11 Matthew Etherington, 10 Marlon Harewood, 25 Bobby Zamora, 26 Shaun Newton, 9 Dean Ashton, 6 Carl Fletcher.

Scorers: Zamora 25, Reo-Coker 32, Etherington 80
MoM: Nigel Reo-Coker
West Ham ended the season: 9th out of 20, with 55 points.

Number: 97	2005-06	FA Cup final
13th May 2006	Liverpool (Cardiff)	Att: 74,000

LIVERPOOL 3 WEST HAM 3

In the same way that West Ham visited Wembley in three successive summers in the 1960s (1964, Preston, FA Cup final; 1965 TSV Munich 1860, Cup-Winners Cup final; 1966 West Germany, World Cup final – well, Moore, Hurst and Peters, in any case), they now found themselves playing at the Millennium Stadium in three successive summers (2004, Palace play-off final; 2005, Preston, play-off final; 2006, Liverpool in the last FA Cup final to be played at Cardiff).

Having made the link with the 1960s, it is sad to say West Ham only won one of their 21st century visits, despite being the better team in all three. The Cup final was perhaps a bonus for Pardew's first Premiership season. He had already led his team to ninth, but now found his side contesting their first FA Cup final for 26 years. What transpired was, in the words of the BBC's John Motson, 'the greatest FA Cup final of all time.'

Pardew stuck with the side that reached Cardiff. Reo-Coker was captain and Hislop, destined to appear in the 2006 World Cup finals for Trinidad & Tobago, continued in goal. The only man who should have been there but wasn't was Hayden Mullins, sent off in a league game with Liverpool and therefore ineligible. That meant good news for West Ham's Welsh international Carl Fletcher, no stranger to the Millennium Stadium, home for all Wales' football internationals.

Lionel Scaloni was involved in the first (and the last) goal. His cross caught out Jamie Carragher, who turned into the back of his own net. Seven minutes later it was 2-0! Etherington's shot was fumbled by Reina, and Dean Ashton converted from close range.

Liverpool's Crouch then had a 'goal' disallowed for offside before their French striker Cisse volleyed Gerrard's pass beyond Hislop. But West Ham still held their lead at half-time.

The second half saw Liverpool step up another gear. Captain Gerrard equalised in the 54th minute when Alonso's free-kick was headed down to him by Crouch. Ten minutes later, one of West Ham's England caps, Paul Konchesky, hit a long probing cross from the left flank which Reina allowed to fly over his shoulder into the top corner. That meant West Ham had enjoyed two goalkeeping errors and an own-goal, and now had a real chance to land a major trophy.

Then Scaloni's second moment, not as memorable as his first. He panicked in defence and gave the ball away. The PA had barely announced the added minutes when Gerrard thundered the ball from 30 yards as cleanly as it was possible to do. On TV the ball flew towards its target at a speed impressive even on the slowest of slow-motion replays. An injury-time equaliser. All the hallmarks of the long-suffering West Ham fan's pain. And they all know that Hammers will lose a penalty shoot-out. They will have to score another goal and win the game in extra-time, or lose the lottery.

And they almost achieve it. Reo-Coker's effort was tipped on to the post by Reina, and with the goal gaping before him the rebound flies wide off Harewood.

Reina's last five minutes proved more crucial than his previous 120, for he loves penalty shoot-outs. Hammers' three subs had arrived in preparation, among them that old hand Teddy Sheringham. If only West Ham could tweak the rules so he could take all five. No one was surprised when Reina saved three of West Ham's kicks, all but Sheringham's. Still, Hammers will be in Europe next year as losing finalists.

West Ham had played in the first ever Wembley FA Cup final in 1923, so if the Australian construction company had done their job as planned and finished the new Wembley in time for the 2006 FA Cup final, would the result have been different?

34 Shaka Hislop, 2 Lionel Scaloni, 5 Anton Ferdinand, 4 Danny Gabbidon, 3 Paul Konchesky, 15 Yossi Benayoun, 6 Carl Fletcher, 20 Nigel Reo-Coker (capt), 9 Dean Ashton, 11 Matthew Etherington, 10 Marlon Harewood, 25 Bobby Zamora, 7 Christian Dailly, 8 Teddy Sheringham.

Scorers: Jamie Carragher 21 (og), Dean Ashton 28, Paul Konchesky 64
MoM: Steven Gerrard
West Ham ended the season: 9th out of 20, with 55 points.

Number: 98	2006-07	Premiership
13th May 2007	Manchester United (a)	Att: 75,927

MANCHESTER UNITED 0 WEST HAM 1

In short, this game proved that football has had its magic squeezed out by money and greed. Alan Pardew had gone, the reasons for his going a book in itself; Icelandic takeovers, the pathological need for a scapegoat, the pathological need for a messiah (Curbishley), Argentinian 'signings', Phil Hall – a man who came and went without ceremony, an inability to win home games, untimely injuries … The list goes on.

Pardew's achievements were promotion and that FA Cup final. Redknapp achieved many things in his seven years at Upton Park, but Pardew managed more, and in less time. Redknapp signed Di Canio and has since won the FA Cup with Portsmouth, but it's difficult to measure these achievements because of other madness plaguing football. Pardew had the two Argentinians forced upon him, with pressure to play them despite their being unfit. In the end it was Curbishley who benefited from a fit Carlos Tevez. Wthout Tevez, West Ham would unquestionably have been relegated, but arguably it was with him that problems first arose.

This was the game immediately after United had claimed the Premier League, so the result was irrelevant in that sense, but to lose in front of their own 70,000+ crowd after being presented with the trophy would reduce Sir Alex Ferguson to apoplexy. The West Ham team formed a guard of honour to welcome the champions onto the pitch.

West Ham needed at least a draw to stay up if results went their way; a win would ensure safety. History has shown that the 'difficult' tasks are often achieved by struggling West Ham sides where avoiding relegation is concerned. The 'impossible', however, away from home, was a tough call.

United knocked the ball around in the opening half-hour, but as half-time approached started making unforced errors and conceding unnecessary corners. Tevez was always a threat to them, and now he broke into the United penalty area, got lucky with the bounce, and slid an opening goal for West Ham.

The second half was predictably backs-to-the-wall. The occasion recalled the Redknapp win in 2001 after Di Canio's goal. Like Di Canio, Tevez had been the foreign import to stir things up. Like in 2001, the Hammers held on to finish an improbable 15th (almost lower mid-table) in Alan Curbishley's first half-season. How much credit could the messiah take? Depends which messiah you mean. If the Argentinian one, then the answer is plenty.

For West Ham, this was certainly their Greatest Escape ever. No one had given them a prayer just a few matches earlier. There was a kerfuffle over the ensuing fortnight as Sheffield United, the unlucky relegated 'next up' on the list, attempted to take the Hammers to a tribunal for playing unregistered and illegal players (Mascherano and Tevez), but their efforts were red-taped long enough to ensure that the results could not be overturned.

The West Ham end-of-season DVD outsold Chelsea's by almost two to one, for it told a tale that could hardly be believed.

1 Robert Green, 2 Lucas Neill (capt), 3 James Collins, 5 Anton Ferdinand, 6 George McCartney, 15 Yossi Benayoun, 20 Nigel Reo-Coker, 24 Mark Noble, 13 Luis Boa-Morte, 25 Bobby Zamora, 32 Carlos Tevez, 18 Jonathan Spector, 10 Marlon Harewood, 17 Hayden Mullins.

Scorer: Carlos Tevez 45
MoM: Carlos Tevez
West Ham ended the season: 15th out of 20, with 41 points.

| Number: 99 | 2007-08 | Premiership |
| 29th December 2007 | Manchester United (h) | Att: 67,000 |

WEST HAM 2 MANCHESTER UNITED 1

Many games at Upton Park over the years have produced results that defy explanation, such as this one. Hammers had struggled to draw against a weak Reading three days earlier, and had been beaten twice in a week at home (in league and cup) by Everton, the first of which denying West Ham a League Cup semi-final appearance for the first time in eighteen years.

United's visit was the first time the sides had met since the last day of 2006-07. The home fixture that season had marked Curbishley's debut as West Ham manager, cheered by a 1-0 win. His goalscorer that day had left for Aston Villa, while his goalscorer from the final game of 2006-07 was now playing for the opposition. Tevez received the warmest ovation when he took to the field.

United were expected to see off the Hammers and push further away from pursuing Chelsea, so when Player of the Season Cristiano Ronaldo headed them ahead after fourteen minutes few were surprised. Indeed, when Spector handled midway through the second half it looked all over bar the whingeing. Ronaldo doesn't miss penalty-kicks (he only missed one in the League all season). Luckily for West Ham, this was the one. He put the ball well wide of Rob Green's post. At that stage in the season Green had faced four league penalties and not been beaten by any of them.

Ten minutes earlier Scott Parker's injury saw him replaced by Anton Ferdinand, returning to the side for the first time since October. It was not long before Ferdinand went up for a Mark Noble corner and headed an unexpected equaliser. It was not the kind of goal Manchester United usually concede. Yet five minutes later the West Ham defence pushed up again, this time for Noble's free-kick, and this time Matthew Upson headed home to put the Hammers in front. Two goals from two set plays; chump stuff, really.

This was only West Ham's third home league win all season. Alex Ferguson was absent from the technical area due to his latest touchline ban, so hadn't been able to direct affairs. He did, though, admit that he did not see the defeat coming. Curbishley, however, was full of praise for West Ham's 'twelfth man', the fans.

1 Robert Green, 2 Lucas Neill (capt.), 18 Jonathan Spector, 6 Matthew Upson, 3 George McCartney, 15 Norberto Solano, 8 Scott Parker, 17 Hayden Mullins, 16 Mark Noble, 7 Freddie Ljungberg, 12 Carlton Cole, 14 John Pantsil, 5 Anton Ferdinand, 9 Dean Ashton.

Scorers: Anton Ferdinand 77, Matthew Upson 82
MoM: Matthew Upson
West Ham ended the season: 10th out of 20, with 49 points.

Number: 100   2007-08   Premiership
15th March 2008   Blackburn Rovers (h)   Att: 34,006

WEST HAM 2 BLACKBURN 1

Alan Curbishley might have dreamed of many honeymoon years ahead after he had presided over the 2006-07 Greatest Escape. Even so, he diced with death over three games the following season, all of which ended up 0-4 defeats. In short, three matches, three defeats, scored none conceded 12. The fact that the first and last of these defeats were against Chelsea and Tottenham should make clear the seriousness of the offence. That at Liverpool was not in the same league of insult. Chelsea had actually routed the Hammers at Upton Park, and it was scant consolation that Frank Lampard got sent off for his foul on Boa Morte. Then, one of the worst Tottenham sides in memory also scored four. West Ham's previous positive goal-difference turned negative seemingly overnight.

These are the sort of times that call for a visit from Blackburn, who have often rescued West Ham from the doldrums over the years. This is partly down to Ludek Miklosko almost single-handedly preventing Manchester United stealing the Premiership title from Blackburn in 1995. Since then, Blackburn sides have repaid the Hammers handsomely.

In 1997-98 it was Rovers who, in the fifth round of the FA Cup, lost a penalty shoot-out at Ewood Park. In 2002-03 it was Blackburn who provided West Ham with their first home win of the season, six months after it had started. In 2006-07 Rovers offered Alan Pardew only his second home league win in three months, and then helped Curbishley's team win a 'goal' from Bobby Zamora that didn't cross the line. So what could Blackburn offer after three 0-4 defeats? Even a draw would do.

West Ham even gave Blackburn a goal start, as was common that season, when Santa Cruz headed in Pedersen's cross. Then came a Norwich old boys' route one effort, with Green's clearance finding Ashton who took the ball past Samba before steering it beyond Brad Friedel.

With a quarter of an hour to go, Curbishley took an untypical gamble. Taking off Parker and Solano, he brought on Mark Noble and the eighteen-year-old youth-team goal sensation Freddie Sears for his debut. Two minutes later Sears fired at Friedel, who was unable to gather cleanly, and the youngster headed in the loose ball.

Despite the days of exorbitant foreign signings and a dearth of home talent, the Hammers had done it again, producing a match winner from amongst their own. Sears had sealed an important victory, in what was only Blackburn's second Premier League defeat of 2008.

1 Robert Green, 2 Lucas Neill (capt), 5 Anton Ferdinand, 18 Jonathan Spector, 3 George McCartney, 15 Norberto Solano, 8 Scott Parker, 17 Hayden Mullins, 7 Freddie Ljungberg, 9 Dean Ashton, 10 Bobby Zamora, 40 Freddie Sears, 16 Mark Noble, 14 John Pantsil.

Scorers: Dean Ashton 39, Freddie Sears 81
MoM: Dean Ashton
West Ham ended the season: 10th out of 20, with 49 points.

Number: 101	2008-09	Premiership
30th August 2008	Blackburn Rovers (h)	Att: 34,500

WEST HAM 4 BLACKBURN 1

West Ham started 2008-09 by officially 'retiring' the No 6 shirt. This was a gesture to the unparalleled achievements of its greatest son and captain, Bobby Moore. The current incumbent, Matthew Upson, himself a West Ham and England defender and occasional club captain, played the opening half of a pre-season friendly for the 'Bobby Moore Cup' against Spain's Villareal in the No 6 shirt before surrendering it at half-time and donning his new squad No 15. This might not seem worthy of record in a book about great West Ham matches, but it aptly demonstrates the kind of symbolic football club that West Ham United continues to be. Later that season they 'retired' the bankrupt sponsors' logo off the shirts to further illustrate the point.

The game against Blackburn, managed by Paul Ince after the departure of Mark Hughes, became 'special' once the fixture was announced. Ince quit West Ham in August 1989 but returned from time to time as a player for Manchester United, Liverpool and Middlesbrough, also missing several opportunities to turn out through mystery 'illnesses' and 'temporary' injuries. To his credit, he conducted press interviews prior to this match. He also realised that, were he to win at Upton Park with his new side Blackburn, he would take them, albeit temporarily, to the top of the Premier League.

This was another chance for Ince to prove himself the 'The Guv'nor' after leaving West Ham under a cloud. He had messed up his first opportunity when coming to Upton Park in May 1995 as a Manchester United player, needing victory to snatch the championship from Blackburn. Thirteen years on, he was presented with another chance to silence his unforgiving East London adversaries.

Curbishley might even have welcomed Ince, having been 'under the cosh' himself for a perceived lack of passion and post-honeymoon blues. Something would have to give; these sides rarely drew..

West Ham enjoyed a headed goal by Calum Davenport from a Julien Faubert corner, and a subsequent scuffed shot from Mark Noble that Chris Samba sliced past keeper Paul Robinson under pressure from Dean Ashton, who subsequently celebrated as if the goal were his. It wasn't.

Jason Roberts, a troublesome striker, pulled a goal back for Rovers after turning his marker Davenport and prodding the ball beyond Green. Six minutes later the dangerous Santa Cruz went off injured, and his replacement Matt Derbyshire had the ball in the net within moments but the effort was disallowed for the most marginal of offsides.

Two minutes into the second half Roveres had another great chance to equalise when Carlton Cole inexplicably threw out two hands to block Steven Reid's free-kick. Hammer of the Year Rob Green had made a habit out of saving penalties the previous season, and did it again with a one-handed stop from Roberts. Green made more saves to preserve West Hams' advantage.

Eventually Blackburn's commitment to chasing an equaliser left them short at the back, and during five minutes injury-time Curbishley's men scored twice, first through a volley by sub Craig Bellamy, making his first appearance of the season, and then a fourth when Cole tapped in with almost the last kick of the game. Both Bellamy and Neill were ex-Rovers players, which must have increased the pain for Blackburn fans.

So, further disappointment at Upton Park for Ince, but the three points saw West Ham leapfrog Blackburn in the table, climbing to the giddy heights of fourth, albeit for 24 hours.

Days later, following the transfer deadline sale of George McCartney to Sunderland, Curbishley quit, stating irreconcilable differences with the board over his role and transfer decision-making. The Blackburn victory, the third of the first three games at Upton Park that season, turned out to be Curbishley's farewell. The new manager would be Gianfranco Zola.

1 Rob Green, 2 Lucas Neill (capt), 8 Scott Parker, 9 Dean Ashton, 11 Matthew Etherington, 12 Carlton Cole, 15 Matthew Upson, 16 Mark Noble, 20 Julien Faubert, 21 Valon Behrami, 27 Calum Davenport, 3 George McCartney, 10 Craig Bellamy, 17 Hayden Mullins.

Scorers: Davenport 12, Samba 20 (og), Bellamy 90, Cole 90
MoM: Carlton Cole
West Ham ended the game: 4th out of 20, with 6 out of 9 points.